WRITERS' AND ARTISTS' RIGHTS

DON GLASSMAN

Basic Benefits and Protections to Authors, Artists, Composers, Sculptors, Photographers, Choreographers and Movie-makers Under

The New American Copyright Law

WRITERS PRESS
Washington, D. C.

PUBLISHED BY WRITERS PRESS
Box 805
2000 Connecticut Avenue • Washington, D. C. 20008

To the Memory of My Parents

Library of Congress Catalog Card No. 77-95457
ISBN 0-931536-01-4

Printed in the United States of America
by National Creative Printing, Inc.
Beltsville, Maryland

Typesetting by
Fowler's Composition, Inc.
Rockville, Maryland

TABLE OF CONTENTS

PREFACE

THIS BOOK aims to inform an ever-widening circle of authors, artists, composers, editors, officials and others who, directly or indirectly, are affected by the amended and revitalized United States Copyright Law (Title 17 of the U.S. Code) which took effect on January 1, 1978, the first major revision since 1909.

The new Act affects all Americans engaged in the art and craft of authorship, that is, the creators of original copyrightable works, as well as the organizations, institutions and industries involved in replicating, diffusing and marketing such works. Additionally the copyright law is of some concern to an enormous public of readers, listeners and spectators.

Basic aspects of Title 17 apply generally to all categories of original authorship, but some provisions of the Act concern only specific copyrightable works. In my limited space I could not detail all the provisions of the new Act, but I enlarge on the application of copyrights to literary works because they are the central core around which other works of authorship were added. The last part of this book concerns the contractual relationships of authors and publishers, with some observations on how they are affected by the new Act.

As revised and amended, Title 17 culminates long years of arduous labor on the part of lawmakers, professionals in the creative arts, leaders in the communications industries and others who collaborated in forging the final document.

The new Act evolved from the long-standing legislation which preceded it, but it extends and amplifies the protection to authors and their heirs. The broader provisions supporting authors' rights give a new direction to copyright philosophy. Moreover the law realistically anticipates technical advances in satellites, computers, laser beams, automation, television, photocopying and printing which may materialize. At the same time it insures the ready access of educators, librarians and non-commercial broadcasters to a vast accumulation of copyrighted treasures.

All such developments represent extensions of the powers granted to Congress by Article One of the Constitution. Exercising that power, Congress enacted the first Copyright Act in 1790.

Culminating a long period of technological change, the 1976 Act was adopted after 15 years of research, debate and negotiation by lawmakers and the principals of organized groups of writers, educators, librarians, broadcasters and professionals in all the creative arts. The responsibilities, obligations and benefits specified in the final Act were arrived at through open hearings and discussions. In every way this far-reaching legislation reflects the wisdom of the democratic process.

1

Part One
History Speaks

All Copyright Systems Emerged from the Communication Arts and Sciences

THE POWER TO COMMUNICATE is a common resource of the lower animals as well as man. Hence we may assume that our anthropoid ancestors, likewise, communicated with each other.

Many millennia ago primitive men engaged in communal hunting and communicated by sounds and gestures, a far cry from the languages and written communications which existed before the tonal alphabet was invented.

Signs, symbols and pictures preceded formalized writing. As used here, "writing" includes the wedge-shaped inscriptions engraved on clay tablets, called cuneiform; and hieroglyphic writing, known to the Egyptians and the Maya.

Leading scholars have traced the roots of writing, seeking to identify its progressive stages of development. Many ancient scripts, carvings, signs and symbols have been deciphered and several dead languages have been restored to life. The Egyptian hieroglyphs have been deciphered but important segments of the Maya glyphs have not yielded their secrets. Nor can we read or understand the symbols painted on pebbles and cobbles at Mas d'Azil in southern France.

In greater Peru writing was unknown until the 16th Century. Knotted and colored cords attached to crossbars served as remembrance devices. The knots and colors reminded "rememberers" of numbers, events and messages. Unfortunately we cannot decipher the quipus today.

The modeling of familiar animals and drawings of hunting scenes were succeeded by pictographic writing wherein conventional signs or pictograms symbolized animals and objects. A number of pictograms found in ancient Sumerian diggings probably represent some of the conventional signs used in pictographic communication.

The later and more complex ideograms represent actions, ideas, qualities and certain objects. Occurring in the Near East, Egypt and early Chinese writings, the imaginative ideograms communicated mainly by suggestion. Chinese ideograms were written in more than 40,000 characters.

THESE DECORATED PEBBLES of various sizes date from the close of the Paleolithic period. Found in caves at Mas d'Azil, in southern France, their meaning remains obscure. They may be just decorative or signify the symbols of private individuals.

THE DIRECT SIMPLICITY of these pictograms suggests that in various parts of the world primitive peoples were observing and imitating nature. Each pictogram is a pictorial word. The animal symbol is Scandinavian, the fish is Chinese and the tree American Indian.

THIS MIGHT BE AN ANIMAL HUNT, a ballet or an expression of the good life observed by a Stone Age artist in Australia.

STONE AGE ARTISTS in Spain drew such pictures on cave walls and rock exposures on mountain sides. This art style resembles pictures found in other regions.

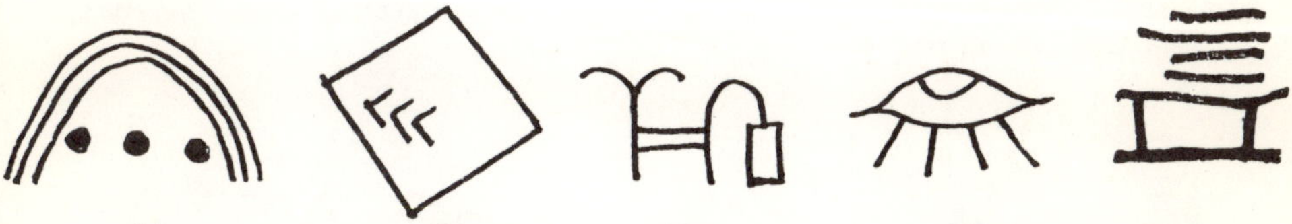

(a) (b) (c) (d) (e)

IN TIME, picture writing became less imitative and more imaginative. The single image evolved into ideograms in which the artist invented and combined symbols to express ideas, actions and qualities. Ideographic writing developed in many regions: (a) an American Indian sign suggests that three days (suns) elapsed under the vault of heaven; (b) this Mesopotamian symbol means "month"; each of the three chevrons represents ten days; (c) an Egyptian ideogram for "writing"; the split reed is tied to an ink bottle; (d) the weeping eye is also from Egypt; (e) the rectangle is the Chinese symbol for mouth and the parallel lines represent vapor.

Coatepec

PHONOGRAMS APPEARED when sign writing was first linked to spoken words, a revolutionary stage in the history of writing. The phonogram at left is the Aztec sign for a town called Coatepec, derived from coatl, meaning "snake" and tepec, meaning "hill". Coatepec is literally the "snake on the hill."

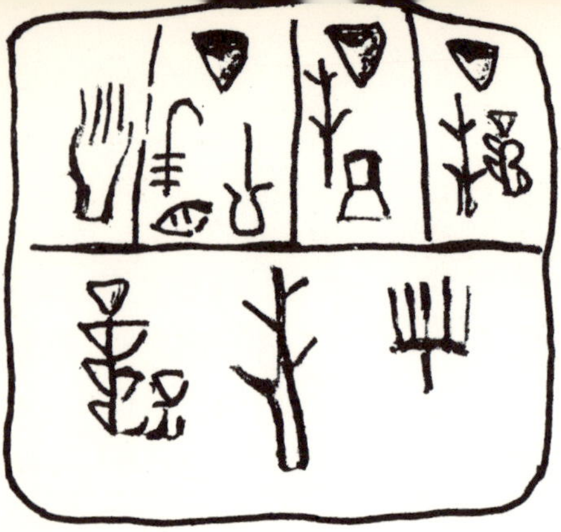

THIS SKETCH, drawn from a stone tablet preserved in the Louvre Museum, dates back to the fourth millennium B.C. and is purported to represent the birth of systematic and conscious writing. These pictographic symbols evolved into cuneiform characters.

THE ANCIENTS IN MESOPOTAMIA left us a rich legacy of their culture because after 3500 B.C. they inscribed characters in clay tablets. The first cuneiform ("wedge-shaped") writing was pictographic but evolved into a phonetic script based on an alphabet.

EGYPTIAN HIEROGLYPHICS appeared about 5000 years ago and persisted until about the fourth century A.D. The characters were chiseled into monumental and funerary inscriptions as well as written on papyrus. French scholar Jean François Champollion deciphered the inscriptions in 1822 through a study of the Rosetta Stone, written in three ancient scripts. He solved the Egyptian puzzle when he realized that the glyphs were phonetic symbols of spoken words, but not alphabetized.

The early stages of sign and symbol writing developed apart from the speech faculty. In some languages the spoken words were equivalent to the visual signs, but for many centuries they were not linked. In the ensuing stage of communications, picturegrams were linked to spoken words to form phonograms. Thus a picture of a boat also represented the spoken word for "boat". Likewise, the image of a man mounted on a horse suggested the spoken word for "horseman". The rebus principle of drawings suggesting word sounds evidently dates back to the age of phonograms.

The syllabary system of writing also evolved from phonograms. Each sign represented a syllable; two and three-syllable words required an equal number of signs.

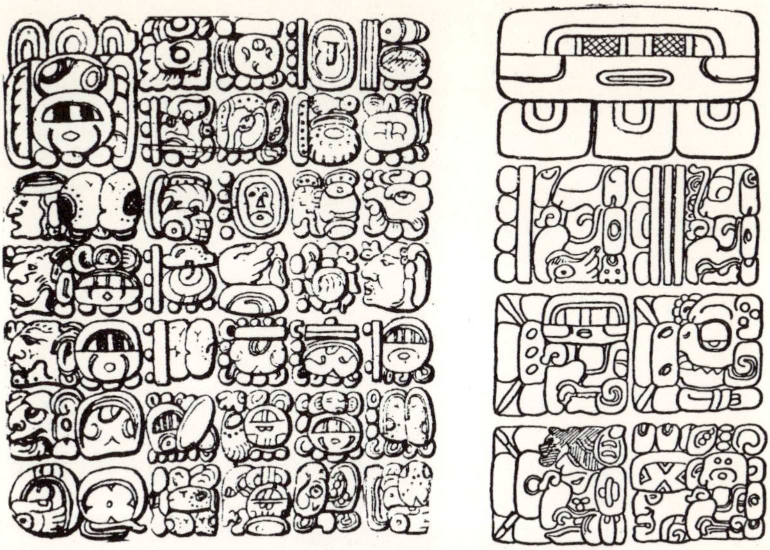

HIEROGLYPHS FROM MAYA LAND

FAR FROM THE OLD WORLD, the isolated Maya and Aztecs in Mesoamerica also developed hieroglyphic writing. Although their hand-made books, or codices, were destroyed by the Spaniards, there is evidence that writing was sacred to their religion and culture. Hieroglyphs chiseled into Maya buildings and monuments occur in great abundance. For the most part, the Maya glyphs remain undeciphered. These early Americans made spectacular advances in astronomy, architecture and mathematics, even inventing a zero symbol.

THIS STRINGED DEVICE, the kipu, was the nearest approach to writing in the great Empire of Peru until the 16th century. It consisted of colored and knotted strings attached to a crossbar. The man shown here may well have been an accountant in the Emperor's household. He was trained to remember, since the kipu's knots and colors served merely to jog or revive his memory of the news or information he must transmit from one relay station to another. Memory systems based on knots and colored cords were used in many parts of the ancient world, even in Greece.

The tonal alphabet, the final and most durable writing system, arrived after many centuries of trial and error. Each letter stands for a single vowel or consonant. Syllabary writing also had signs for single vowels, but the invention of a single sign for every consonant was the epic achievement of the tonal alphabet because, in truth, every consonant sound is joined to a vowel, as in "L", pronounced "EL".

All the tonal alphabets sprang from a Semitic alphabet which arose in Palestine, Syria and Phoenicia. The oldest known alphabetical inscriptions are estimated to date back to the 17th century B.C. The sacred scriptures of the Hindus, Moslems and the Old Testament in Hebrew were derived from the original Semitic alphabet, consisting of 32 letters written horizonally from right to left.

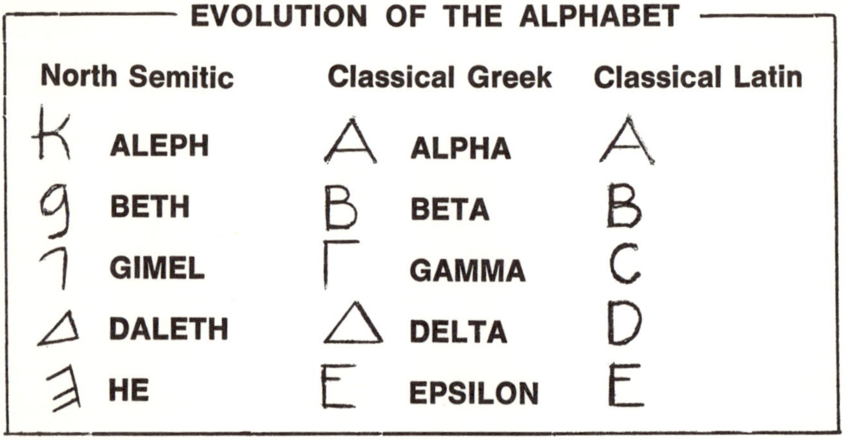

ANCIENT PHOENICIA, embracing Palestine, Syria and Sinai, appears to have been the birthplace of alphabetic writing. At the site of Byblos, a French scholar found a North Semitic alphabet estimated to be 3100 years old. This was evidently the basic alphabet whose 20 consonants evolved into new signs which became ancestral to all modern alphabets. The Greeks added vowels when they adopted alphabetic writing. Alphabets range from 20 to 30 letters which can express an almost endless number of spoken words. The non-alphabetic writing systems may require thousands of ideogram characters. The recent discovery of early "Canaanite" scripts have now pushed back the alphabet's invention to 3700 years ago.

Phonetic alphabets attracted people to writing and also accounted for a rising interest in learning to read. Before the printing revolution, hand-written manuscripts bound into books were the principal literary fare. They were quite costly and scarce. Readers bought, borrowed and bartered them. Neither the contents nor the authors were protected by laws.

Johann Gutenberg's invention of the printing press, about 1437, sowed the seeds of copyright protection. It touched off an explosion in writing, reading and reproduction by diffusing a knowledge of history, religion, art, science and literature to scholars and a literate public. Masterpieces, from the Bible to the writings of Leonardo da Vinci, Chaucer, Cervantes and Dante, found their way into print and wide circulation. More and more books appeared in translations. Printers, publishers, and book dealers profited from this thriving trade, but the authors earned least of all.

The Renaissance was well under way by 1476 when the city of Venice initiated so-called "privileges" or limited monopolies to encourage the printing of certain books. Other countries adopted this plan, motivated chiefly by an opportunity to enrich the royal treasuries with fees from printers for monopoly rights. Moreover it enabled rulers to censor or reject what they disliked. This system prevailed on the Continent for some 200 years, but authors derived no benefit from it.

Johann Gutenberg

THE CLASSIC AND SHADOWY JOHANN GUTENBERG, whose name is spelled in various ways, may well be termed the Great Communicator and Emancipator of the human race for his invention of movable type. Simple in itself, it opened the floodgates of learning and knowledge in all languages and freed humanity from age-old shackles of ignorance and illiteracy. All the world pays homage to the printer's printer. Every school, college and university, every book-filled library represents a memorial to Gutenberg's achievement.

ARTIST'S CONCEPTION of Gutenberg inspecting the first proof sheet.

MONUMENTS MEMORIALIZE JOHANN GUTENBERG'S INVENTION of a punch at the end of a steel rod for casting individual letters of metal type from a copper matrix. This ingenious tool made it possible to produce and print with movable type, perhaps the greatest contribution to the art of communication and the democratization of knowledge since the invention of the alphabet.

Homes, libraries and universities cherish works printed by movable type, but the vital records of Gutenberg's personal life and his achievements as a scholar, printer and inventor are scarce and vague. Even the year of his birth, approximately 1398, is disputed. He died about 1468. What we know is that Gutenberg, like many innovators, was embroiled in disputes and litigations. The meaningful word "printing" first appeared in a court record involving Gutenberg.

Movable type, that is, type that can be used and reused, was the basic difference between Gutenberg's invention and the fixed characters, or ideograms, carved on wood slabs by Japanese and Chinese printers who preceded Gutenberg by six or more centuries.

Gutenberg is the "printer's printer", not only for his inventions but for the quality of his graphic artistry. Today, more than 500 years after his death, his style and craftsmanship are universal standards for master printers, many of whom doubt that his expertise will ever be surpassed. Countless visitors have been awed by Gutenberg's three-volume edition of the Latin Bible, printed on vellum, proudly displayed at the Library of Congress. These tomes were acquired, along with 3000 other rare volumes, for $1.5 million dollars, funded by Congress.

THREE-VOLUME EDITION of the Gutenberg Bible, printed on vellum and owned by the Library of Congress, is among the world's most valuable books. A Gutenberg Bible printed on paper ranges in value from $1.8 million to $2.8 million. The vellum specimens are worth considerably more.

A SAMPLE LINE OF GENESIS as it appears in the vellum edition.

THIS PROBABLY REPRESENTS the type of print shop used by Gutenberg.

About 1566, England's Queen Mary I fostered a tight censorship by issuing monopoly licenses to some printers and meting out punishment for violations. Her licensing system survived until 1694 after which plagiarism and piracy flourished. Authors and printers protested loudly and in 1710, in the reign of Queen Anne, Parliament responded with a copyright law that was imperfect yet it attained far-reaching renown because it invoked revolutionary principles that were adopted around the globe. The Statute of Queen Anne recognized authors as the fountainhead of copyright protection and provided them with a term of exclusivity for benefitting from their works.

Anno Octavo

Annæ Reginæ.

An Act for the Encouragement of Learning, by Vesting the Copies of Printed Books in the Authors or Purchasers of such Copies, during the Times therein mentioned.

Whereas Printers, Booksellers, and other Persons have of late frequently taken the Liberty of Printing, Reprinting, and Publishing, or causing to be Printed, Reprinted, and Published Books, and other Writings, without the Consent of the Authors or Proprietors of such Books and Writings, to their very great Detriment, and too often to the Ruin of them and their Families: For Preventing therefore such Practices for the future, and for the Encouragement of Learned Men to Compose and Write useful Books; May it please Your Majesty, that it may be Enacted, and be it Enacted by the Queens most Excellent Majesty, by and with the Advice and Consent of the Lords Spiritual and Temporal, and Commons in this present Parliament Assembled, and by the Authority of the same, That from and after the Tenth Day of April, One thousand seven hundred and ten, the Author of any Book or Books already Printed, who hath not Transferred to any other the Copy or Copies of such Book or Books, Share or Shares thereof, or the Bookseller or Booksellers, Printer or Printers, or other Person or Persons, who hath or have Purchased or Acquired the Copy or Copies of any Book or Books, in order to Print or Reprint the same, shall have the sole Right and Liberty of Printing such Book and Books for the Term of One and twenty Years, to Commence from the said Tenth Day of April, and no longer; and that the Author of any Book or Books already Composed and not Printed and Published, or that shall hereafter be Composed, and his Assignee, or Assigns, shall have the sole Liberty of Printing and Reprinting such Book and Books for the Term of Fourteen

6 Ttt 2 teen

FIRST PAGE OF THE STATUTE OF QUEEN ANNE

MOST BIOGRAPHERS pass over the fact that Queen Anne (1665-1714) personifies a Statute that set a pattern for most of the copyright laws now in existence. In truth, she is better known for Queen Anne's lace and Queen Anne period furniture.

Princess Anne was the daughter of James, Duke of York, who became James II in 1685. She mounted the throne in 1702 and ruled with compassion. During her reign England enjoyed agricultural prosperity and in 1707 she was instrumental in formally uniting England and Scotland under the name of Great Britain. She also concluded the Treaty of Utrecht which gave Gibraltar to England.

Queen Anne was the last of the Stuart monarchs. In her eagerness to produce an heir, she gave birth 17 times, but all her offspring died in infancy except the Duke of Gloucester who succumbed at age 11.

The above painting was presented to the College of William and Mary in Williamsburg, Virginia, by the Drapers' Company of London.

Authors' Rights Reenforced

The Statute clearly sets forth an author's inherent title to original work and induced comparative order out of the corruption and piracy that had beset the publishing industry ever since William Caxton established England's first printing plant in Westminster.

The law granted authors exclusive ownership along with other rights pertaining to the use and sale of literary property. It forbade infringements and provided for the registration of original works in an official archive — basic features in the copyright codes of many nations today.

The preamble of Queen Anne's Statute states plainly what motivated Parliament to enact this legislation. It was designed to correct a situation wherein —

> **". . . Printers, Booksellers and other Persons have of late frequently taken the Liberty of Printing, Reprinting and Publishing, or causing to be Printed, Reprinted and Published Books, and other Writings, without the Consent of the Authors or Proprietors of such Books and Writings, to their very great Detriment, and too often to the Ruin of them and their Families:**
>
> **"For Preventing therefore such Practices for the future, and for the Encouragement of Learned Men to Compose and Write useful Books; May it please Your Majesty, that it may me enacted by the Queens Most Excellent Majesty. . . ."**

The State of Publishing in Colonial America

In pre-revolutionary time, the American Colonies were virtually without ways or means for producing and distributing books, much less to think about such an esoteric subject as copyrights. A few titles were published in Philadelphia, New York and Boston but scarcely enough to serve the population. England and the Continent filled the needs of scholars and universities. The Bible was often the only book in American households.

The disruption and havoc during the independence struggle and the hard years which followed it discouraged writers and hindered the development of anything but local newspapers.

It is difficult to say how long the new Republic might have floundered by relying on imported reading matter were it not for a son born in 1758 to devout parents in West Hartford, Connecticut. As a teenager Noah Webster and his brothers helped his parents run the family farm. Each morning the brothers trudged four miles to a one-room schoolhouse and read the weekly *Connecticut Courant* published in Hartford. Noah's hunger for learning manifested itself early. He attended Yale College where a library of 2500 books absorbed his interest. Among other subjects, he studied the Latin, Greek and Hebrew classics.

THE

VVHOLE

BOOKE OF PSALMES

Faithfully

TRANSLATED *into* ENGLISH

Metre.

Whereunto is prefixed a discourse declaring not only the lawfullnes, but also the necessity of the heavenly Ordinance of singing Scripture Psalmes in the Churches of God.

Coll. III.

Let the word of God dwell plenteously in you, in all wisdome, teaching and exhorting one another in Psalmes, Himnes, and spirituall Songs, *singing to the Lord with grace in your hearts.*

Iames V.

If any be afflicted, let him pray, and if any be merry let him sing psalmes.

Imprinted

1640

THE FIRST BOOK PRINTED IN THE AMERICAN COLONIES

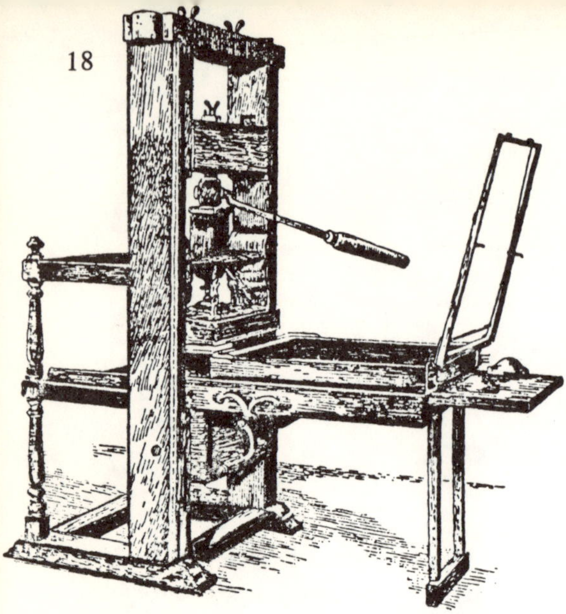

THIS MODEL OF A WOODEN PRINTING PRESS, imported from England, is like the press used by Stephen Day to print "The Whole Booke of Psalmes," in 1640, the first book published in Colonial America.

After he was graduated from Yale, he studied law while teaching school. Then his career took several directions. He abandoned teaching and completed writing *The American Spelling Book* at age 25. When Noah submitted his Speller to various college professors for comment, they winced and shrugged. It was unorthodox and of no use in college curricula. Undismayed, he cast about for a publisher, only to discover that the nearest thing to a book publisher in his native land was a printer; and he soon learned that there were no laws in all the Republic to protect an author's work from piracy and plagiarism.

Young Webster lacked funds to finance the printing. What he did not lack was a conviction, based on his legal studies, that all labor would be lost unless he could protect his work from infringement. In what appeared to be a foolhardy venture, he armed himself with introductions and a book manuscript and traveled by stagecoach to various State capitals where he lobbied with such persuasive eloquence that the legislatures of six States adopted copyright laws.

The First American Copyright Laws

Connecticut acted first, in 1783, followed by Massachusetts, Maryland, New Jersey, New Hampshire and Rhode Island. Of course, the lawmakers passed different versions, but they were based principally on England's Statute of Queen Anne. Let it be remembered, however, that Noah Webster originated and set in motion an American copyright system which gave a small measure of protection to all contemporary writers as well as to himself.

After that, all Webster needed was a publisher. In the young Republic public libraries, bookstores and publishers were almost as rare as millionaires. He was too poor to pay a printer, so with character-

AUTHOR, PATRIOT, PHILOLOGIST and founder of the American copyright system, Noah Webster shaped the universal English language by defining its words. Portrait at left shows him in the prime of life; painting at right, by Edwin B. Child, shows how he appeared in his later years.

WEBSTER'S FAMOUS BLUE-BACK SPELLING BOOK, first published in 1783, served five generations of Americans and made an impact on family life that was second only to the Bible. The number of printed copies approached 100 million.

istic audacity Webster persuaded the owners of the *Connecticut Courant* to print 5000 copies of his speller on speculation, but they held him accountable for all costs if the book failed to sell.

In its blue cloth cover, the 119-page Speller constituted an elementary declaration of independence in language and literature. It was a potpourri of geography, science, morality, patriotism, progressive spelling, fables like "The Boy That Stole Apples" and a concise "History of the Creation of the World" in 220 well-chosen words.

Priced at one shilling and tuppence (about 30 cents), it gathered attention slowly, exhausting the first edition in nine months. It made friends among adults as well as children. One million copies were sold in the first ten years. Thereafter it took off like a comet and within Webster's lifetime the sales approached 25 million copies, providing a modest livelihood for himself and family while he toiled on his massive dictionary. "Modest" is the correct word for Webster's royalty of one-half cent per copy sold; 200 copies of the Speller yielded exactly one dollar in royalty.

By raft, wagon train, canoe and horseback, the bluebacked Speller traveled across the continent and before it was superseded by McGuffey's Eclectic Readers, an estimated 100 million copies had been sold.

To appreciate the impact of the Speller we must bear in mind the physical and cultural isolation of America's settlements, villages and communities, linked only by stagecoach and wagon. People of diverse origins wrung a living from the soil. Lacking communication systems, trained teachers and reading matter, they corrupted grammar, pronunciation and spelling. Webster taught them to say *Indian* for *injun, ask* for *ax, chimney* for *chimbly* and *getting* for *gittin'*. At the same time he approved Yankee idioms and words like *chore* and *whittle.* From sea to sea, the blue reader instructed young and old to speak and think in American English.

His Speller was Webster's appetizer for larger undertakings. While pamphleteering and lecturing on political, social and economic themes and striving to correct atrocious speech habits heard everywhere, he preached the twin ideals of political unity and the full freedom of American nationality. He also pursued an enduring interest in linguistics and philology, exalting his power over words and their meaning.

In Webster's critical reading of the British lexicographers, he discovered errors and shortcomings. Few men of his generation would dare to challenge or lecture the British authorities, especially Dr. Samuel Johnson, who habitually sat in judgment on profound subjects.

How could a schoolteacher from rural America reproach the eminent Dr. Johnson? The question should be reversed because Webster was knowledgeable in 20 classic and modern languages; he had lec-

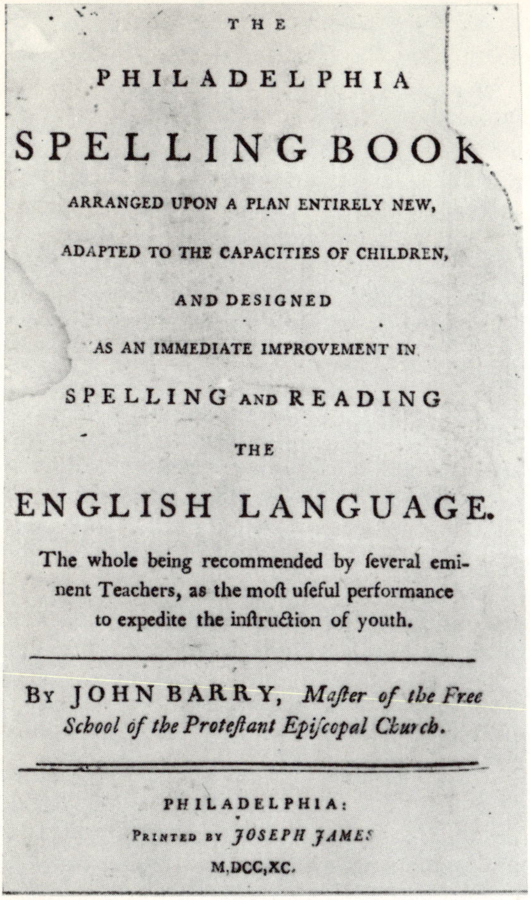
THE

PHILADELPHIA

SPELLING BOOK

ARRANGED UPON A PLAN ENTIRELY NEW,

ADAPTED TO THE CAPACITIES OF CHILDREN,

AND DESIGNED

AS AN IMMEDIATE IMPROVEMENT IN

SPELLING AND READING

THE

ENGLISH LANGUAGE.

The whole being recommended by ſeveral eminent Teachers, as the moſt uſeful performance to expedite the inſtruction of youth.

By JOHN BARRY, *Maſter of the Free School of the Proteſtant Epiſcopal Church.*

PHILADELPHIA:
PRINTED BY *JOSEPH JAMES*
M,DCC,XC.

THE PHILADELPHIA SPELLING BOOK, by schoolmaster John Barry, is a landmark in American culture and history. It was the first book to receive the protection of a copyright under Federal law, in 1790, a time when spelling books were in vogue.

tured on economics, politics and history; had written books on many subjects. Moreover, he discovered flaws and omissions in Dr. Johnson's dictionary, which served readers less and less, whereas Webster's authority soared. By way of asserting America's intellectual progress, Webster leveled barbs at Dr. Johnson's definitions.

About 1807 he intensified his studies in lexicography and soon was in the throes of creating an American dictionary of the English language, a task that held him captive for about 20 years. He involved himself in tracing the roots of words and the evolution of languages, in formulating an etymological philosophy. He also searched European libraries. And in his own hand, he penned the definitions of 70,000 words.

He composed the last entries in 1828 and soon the manuscript was cast into metal type. Critics and the public acclaimed this work, but America was not the only beneficiary. Webster's terms and definitions became standard usage in the English-speaking world.

Thus he laid a new foundation for the English language and bound it to the people of America as an arbiter of speech and literature and the symbol of a nation engrossed in creative learning. It represented his promise to achieve "a new species of independence."

His language belongs to the masses, to the masters of prose and oratory. It shapes our patterns of speech and molds our thoughts. Whoever esteems the virility and versatility of English, whoever employs its powers of communication and cherishes its literature, owes a debt to Noah Webster — everybody's teacher, the founder of our copyright system and author of the American Dictionary, a man to honor and remember.

The First Federal Copyrights

All of the 13 original American States except Delaware adopted copyright systems between 1783 and 1789. They failed because neither authorship nor publishing could adapt to a dozen different and overlapping laws. Only a national copyright system could serve the public interest.

On May 11, 1790, about 14 years after proclaiming independence, the United States Congress enacted its first copyright law, providing protection for books, maps and charts for a term of 14 years and a renewal term for another 14 years. Ten days later the first copyright certificate was issued for the *Philadelphia Spelling Book.*

According to copyright records, Philadelphia was the literary capital of the United States. During the first decade of Federal copyright, Pennsylvania was credited with 262 entries, Massachusetts with 189, New York with 85, Virginia with 14 and Maine with six, a total of 556 copyrights.

The legal authority for copyright appears in Article One of the Constitution, adopted in 1789:

> **"The Congress shall have power to promote the progress of science and useful arts, by securing for limited times to authors and inventors the exclusive right to their respective writings and discoveries."**

By providing statutory protection for the primacy and exclusivity of ownership, the first Federal copyright Act rests firmly on the Statute of Queen Anne. In its early years, the Act did not assuage the hardships and poverty which most writers endured.

By modern standards, the earnings of famous 19th century writers were extremely lean. Edgar Allen Poe lived in the shadow of poverty. Hawthorne spent years at literary hackwork and odd jobs. Walt Whitman could not sustain himself by writing verse alone. Many more writers who enriched the human mind and spirit received low pay for creative achievements. Their works passed into the public domain and were exploited by strangers.

From its inception, the Federal act emphasized the protection of an author's copyright and his right to benefit from it. Incentives written into the American law, as in the copyright codes of other nations, were designed to stimulate and encourage individual creativity and the diffusion of knowledge to the public.

The Meaning of Copyright

In its simplest form, the word *copyright* exemplifies the intent and purpose of numerous statutes. Its etymology suggests that *copyright* has a double meaning: first, *the right to copy* and second, *the right to control.* In French (*droit d'auteur*), German (*Urheberrecht*) and Spanish (*derechos de autor*) have a common sense, that is *an author's rights,* whence I derive *Writers' and Artists' Rights,* the title of this book.

In its first major revision of the copyright law, in 1831, Congress added music to the list of protected works and lengthened the first term of copyright to 28 years. Dramatic rights were added in 1856 and photographs in 1865.

The second major revision took place in 1870. Twenty-one years later Congress authorized the establishment of copyright relations with foreign countries. In 1897 the Copyright Office became a separate agency of the Library of Congress. In 1909, during the third major revision of the Act, the renewal term of a copyright was extended from 14 to 28 years. Five years later, the United States joined other Hemisphere republics adhering to the Pan American Copyright Convention.

In 1947 the copyright law was merged into the positive law as Title 17 of the United States Code and it remains there to this day. Eight years later, the Universal Copyright Convention came into force in the United States. On October 19, 1976, President Ford signed the fourth general revision of the copyright law, taking effect on January 1, 1978. This last revision projects far-reaching changes and concerns all persons engaged in authorship; it extends and strengthens the protection to fixed but unpublished writings and recordings and defends the rights of originating authors, composers, artists, photographers, sculptors and their heirs.

Official Seal of the Copyright Office

THE NEW SPIRIT OF COMMUNICATIONS

Albert Robida Designed the Future

LATE IN THE 19TH CENTURY, Albert Robida (1848-1926) the editor and illustrator of *La Caricature,* amused Paris with "impossible" inventions and scenes of life in the 20th century, which he named "The Electric Age."

It is difficult to characterize Robida. He was called a visionary artist, a philosopher, humorist, historian and illustrator. He was all that and more.

As a youth he had served an illustrated weekly as a war correspondent and sketch artist in the Franco-Prussian War of 1870. His clairvoyance soon appeared after he founded *La Caricature* where his portrayals of social, scientific and political events startled and entertained his readers. Now we know that his predictions had overtones of satire, cynicism and truth. As a graphic commentator on the human condition, Robida had few peers. Many of his prophecies concerned the press and other communications media.

He mused and speculated on the telephone invention soon after it was announced by Alexander Graham Bell. But he went beyond wired telephony and introduced some uncanny pictures and ideas on art, literature, drama, radio and television. None of his contemporaries revealed the promise and potential of electronic communication with

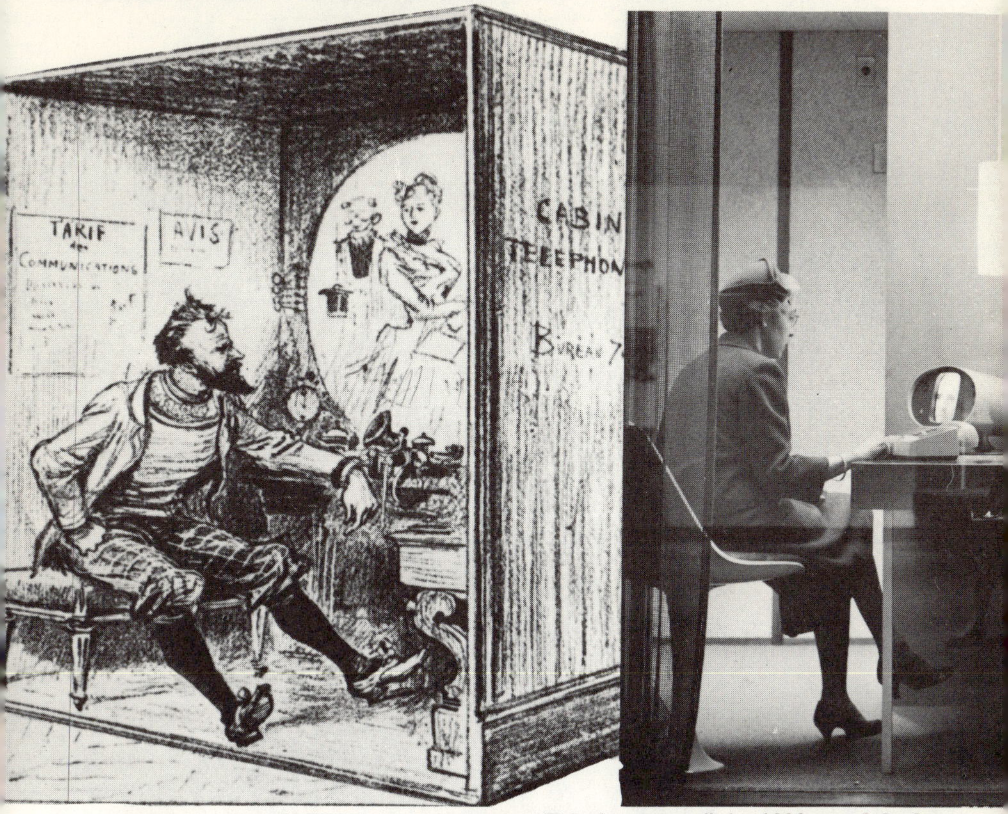

ROBIDA CONCEIVED the big-screen "Telephonoscope" in 1883, on left, but A.T.&T. calls today's miniature sound-and-sight device a Picturephone.

greater clarity or insight, although he was vague about how sounds and pictures could be transmitted through space. His radio and television illustrations appeared in the early 1880's. Perhaps overwhelmed by his own speculations, he concluded solemnly, "Science is like a flood, spreading evenly over the globe, placing everyone on the same plane, so to speak."

Few of Robida's readers considered his schemes and fancies anything more serious than the follies of a Rube Goldberg. His graphic art flowed from an agile pen and lively imagination mingled with a Puckish wit.

Like Jules Verne, a contemporary novelist, Robida unmasked the future, but with an awesome reality, confirming the Chinese proverb, "One picture is worth a thousand words." Significantly, the French Society of Humorists paid its homage and devotion to Robida at his funeral rites.

TRAMWAY PASSENGERS enjoy a wide selection of cultural entertainment.

BROADCASTERS voice commentaries, critiques and the news.

THE TELEPHONE bridges a gap in space between a suitor and sweetheart.

NIGHT VIEW of the "Telephonographic Journal", L'Epoque, one of Robida's most perceptive bits of divination. A press, television and advertising complex, L'Epoque attracts spectators with international television. The moon above reminds us that global television today depends upon "satellites".

Samuel F. B. Morse

Thomas A. Edison

Famous Inventors in th

SAMUEL F. B. MORSE WAS THE TRUE PIONEER OF ELECTRICAL COMMUNICATION. An artist by profession, he wandered through the New England states and painted portraits for a few dollars each. In his free time he tinkered with possible inventions.

He had studied electricity at Yale and when he lacked clients for portraits, he sketched plans involving electrical communication. On becoming a professor of painting at New York University, he met Alfred Vail, a gifted student and model-maker. They formed a partnership and Vail soon designed and built instruments which were quite similar to modern devices. The first signals transmitted by these instruments consisted of numerals. Morse improved that system by inventing a dot-and-dash code which enabled them to transmit figures and letters in the alphabet.

Their invention met with interest and resistance but most people considered it a sort of toy of no practical use. Morse received a United States patent in 1840 but was turned down by various European countries.

At length Congress appropriated $30,000 for a test line between Washington and Baltimore. The line was completed in May 1844 and More wrote the first message, saying, "What hath God wrought?"

The Morse-Vail telegraph was a technical success but could not pay its way. Congress appropriated another $8000. Finally, with success, came the inevitable litigation.

Many small telegraph companies were formed and in 1856 they were consolidated into the Western Union system which soon inaugurated a coast-to-coast service.

In later years honors were heaped upon Marsh worldwide. In 1858 a group of European countries granted him a 400,000 franc annuity.

Emile Berliner

Guglielmo M. Marconi

Communications Hall of Fame

SOME INVENTORS ARE INSPIRED BY VISIONS AND DREAMS, but Thomas A. Edison, the most practical of inventors, was inspired by thinking of what people needed, then went about creating it.

Self-inspired and self-taught, much of Edison's fame rests on a dogged persistence in pursuing practical solutions. Many of his 1400 or more patents gave major impetus to the communication arts and sciences and helped to establish light and heavy industries which sustain the world's economic and technical advancement.

He is credited with fundamental inventions in sound and picture recording, electric power generation, transmission and lighting, as well as hundreds of auxiliary devices. His patents covered telephony, telegraphy and motion picture photography and projection.

He crammed his notebooks full of ideas and sketches. He taught himself the Morse Code and became a railroad telegrapher, ridding his depot of rats by electrocuting them.

Edison sold his first major invention, a stock ticker, for $40,000. Then he accelerated an automatic telegraph system from 50 to 1000 words per minute. Between 1869 and 1871 he received 20 patents for telegraphic devices alone.

In 1878 he invented the phonograph, a hollow cylinder coated with tinfoil. As he sang, a needle etched corresponding vibrations on the tinfoil. His dictaphone invention was an offspring of the phonograph. By 1879 he had developed an incandescent carbon filament, followed by an electric power generating plant on Manhattan Island.

In his motion picture experiments, Edison photographed dancers, boxers and actors on a continuous film strip. One of his last projects was a device to synchronize voices and music with motion pictures.

EMILE BERLINER, INVENTOR OF THE MICROPHONE, TELEPHONE TRANSMITTER AND PHONOGRAPH DISC, emigrated from Germany to the United States in 1870 at age 19. During the panic of 1873 he sold glue, clothing and gave German language lessons.

Without a formal education in science, he studied borrowed books on electricity and acoustics. Despite all handicaps, he patented a number of fundamental inventions which won him distinction in the communication sciences. He was also a recognized authority in acoustic engineering.

In Berliner's flat phonograph discs, which superseded Edison's waxed cylinders, the sound vibrations were recorded and played back by lateral movements of the needle. His method of stamping out duplicate disc recordings led to the establishment of the Berliner Gramophone Co., which developed into the Victor Talking Machine Co.

GUGLIELMO M. MARCONI (1874-1937) an Italian physicist and electrical engineer, was born just two years after Morse died. As a young man Marconi carried on pioneering experiments with electro-magnetic waves, gradually increasing the distance for transmitting telegraphic signals through the ether. His work was, therefore, a logical sequel to the Morse system of wired telegraphy.

Confining himself to wireless telegraphy, Marconi gradually extended the range of his long-wave signals from a few hundred feet to several miles. Subsequently he sent a radio telegraph signal nine miles and still another signal was received by a warship 12 miles from the mainland. In 1898 he extended the range to 18 miles with the first commercial wireless message, aptly called a "Marconigram."

Switching from longwave to shortwave signalling, Marconi demonstrated that he could send radio signals hundreds of miles. In 1901 he achieved his goal of sending a shortwave telegraphic signal across the Atlantic Ocean, the initial step leading to the global transmission of voices, music and pictures, a commonplace today. In 1909 Marconi shared the Nobel Prize for his work in developing wireless telegraphy.

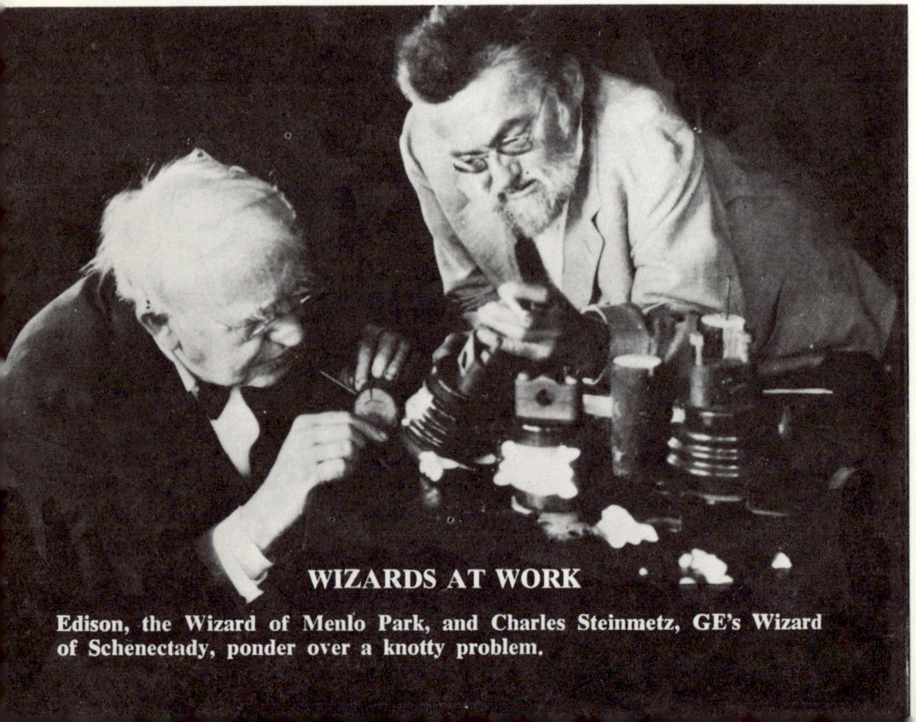

WIZARDS AT WORK

Edison, the Wizard of Menlo Park, and Charles Steinmetz, GE's Wizard of Schenectady, ponder over a knotty problem.

BELL INAUGURATING SERVICE from New York to Chicago in 1892

A VOICE ON THE TELEPHONE DID NOT EXIST UNTIL MARCH 10, 1876, when Alexander Graham Bell accidentally spilled some acid and called to his assistant, "Mr. Watson, come here, I want to see you." Watson rushed in saying, "I heard every word distinctly!" Bell's voice had been transmitted over a wire.

Bell appears to have inherited a family interest in speech, hearing and invention. Both his father and grandfather taught and experimented with a language of sound symbols which they called "visible speech."

Young Bell had received most of his education at home. His studies of speech, elocution and the physiology of the ear and experiments with electrical conductors led to a position at the Boston School for the Deaf. His dedicated work there sparked the idea of "talking telephones." After the initial success of an accidental call, Bell demonstrated "long distance" telephony with an eight-mile transmission and in 1877 he founded the Bell Telephone Co.

Subsequently he was obliged to defend his telephone patent in more than 600 law suits. He survived this ordeal and won recognition as the chief inventor of the device still linked to his name.

In 1880 European nations bestowed the Volta Prize of 50,000 francs on Bell for his work in telephony. Bell's catholic interests involved him in other inventions as well as in aviation and sheepherding.

OCEAN-TO-OCEAN TELEPHONY became a reality after crews of weather-beaten men raised 130,000 telephone poles, strung 13,600 miles of wire and hoisted a flag at the Nevada-Utah line on June 17, 1914. When service began in January, 1915, a cross-country call cost $20.70.

THE LIQUID TELEPHONE, first to carry the voice of Alexander Graham Bell, and model of the touchtone 'phone.

2

Introducing the New Act

Without Writing, Culture is Forever Lost; with Writing, Culture is Preserved and, Through Copyright, Protected

THE YEAR 1976 marked America's Bicentennial, a fitting occasion to announce a new era of free and creative authorship through an amended and updated copyright law. President Ford's signature legalized the 1976 Act, ending a 67-year term for the old act.

The new Act recognizes and adapts to revolutionary technological changes that have taken place in the last three-quarters of a century, adding radio, TV, radiotelephony, laser beams, photocopying and satellite communication — strong spurs to creative endeavors. There was a corresponding expansion in authorship as new recruits swelled the professional ranks. From all appearances, writers still write to earn a living, to report and analyze human affairs, as well as to express personal convictions and satisfy an urge to create and achieve renown. More than ever, publishers remain dedicated businessmen motivated by profit incentives and opportunities in the marketplace.

In a practical sense, authors and publishers are complementary figures; they are essential to each other and both are essential to a literature public. As principals in joint ventures, they share certain risks but generally the profits are not shared equally.

WHY COPYRIGHT?

BECAUSE COPYRIGHT PROVIDES EXCLUSIVE RIGHTS to reproduce specific material, it is, by definition, a monopoly.

The monopoly is given because it serves to advance artistic, intellectual and social development. Without these benefits to society as a whole, granting copyrights would be disadvantageous. In designing a fair copyright law, a proper balance must be struck between those conflicting values.

Copyrighting as a monopolistic practice can only be justified to the extent it serves the public good. That is why the Constitution insists that it be secured only "for limited times."

—Congressman Robert F. Drinan of Massachusetts,
Member of the Copyright Subcommittee,
House Committee on the Judiciary

"FIRSTS" IN PUBLISHING AND COPYRIGHT

868 A.D. — Wang Chieh published the first known printed book, *The Diamond Sutra,* a Buddhist scripture dealing with the "non-existence of all things." It consists of six large sheets of text and one sheet of woodcut illustrations, pasted together. It was printed from wood blocks.

1476 — William Caxton set up the first printing plant in England at Westminster and in the following year he printed *The Dictes and Savengis of the Philosophores,* the first printed and dated book to appear in England.

1638 — The first printing press was imported to the American colonies by Reverend Jose Glover. After his death, Stephen Day printed 1700 copies of *The Whole Booke of Psalmes* in 1640.

1710 — The Statute of Queen Anne enacted by Parliament: the first systematic and conclusive legislation concerning the ownership of literary property and centerpiece of British and American copyright laws. Mentioned more frequently in courts of law than any other enabling legislation.

January 8, 1783 — The General Court of Connecticut enacted the first American copyright statute, titled "an Act for the Encouragement of Literature and Genius", whose leading sponsor and advocate was lexicographer Noah Webster. The first copyrighted book was *Captain James Cook's Last Voyage.*

March 10, 1783 — The Continental Congress authorized the formation of a committee "to consider the most proper means of cherishing genius and the useful arts by securing to the authors or publishers of new books their property in such works."

May 31, 1790 — Congress enacted the first Federal copyright law — "An Act for the Encouragement of Learning", requiring the deposit of a copy of the work with the Secretary of State. Ten days later the first Federal copyright was issued to John Barry, author of *The Philadelphia Spelling Book.*

September 16, 1955 — The Universal Copyright Convention was drafted in Geneva in August 1952, ratified by tht United States September 6, 1952 and came into force September 16, 1955.

January 1, 1978 — The 1976 Copyright Act, the first major revision in 67 years, became law. Among its numerous "firsts" are: the single non-renewable copyright, good for the life of the author plus 50 years; the first Copyright Royalty Tribunal; the first statutory recognition of "fair use" and the first National Television and Radio Archives.

January 3, 1978 — The first book manuscript registered by the United States Copyright Office was *Writers' and Artists' Rights* by Don Glassman.

THE TERMINOLOGY OF COPYRIGHTS

(Definitions Based on U.S. Copyright Law)

AUTHORS are the creators of original works such as literary, musical, pictorial, sculptural, dance works and sight or sound recordings.

AUTHORSHIP refers to the skill, knowledge, ability or talent to produce originally and creatively in a fixed form certain tangible works. These include:

Literary works
Musical works, including accompanying words
Dramatic works, including accompanying music
Pantomime and choreographic works
Pictorial, graphic and sculptural works
Motion pictures and other audiovisual works
Sound recordings

COPYRIGHT is the legal protection afforded to original works of authorship fixed in any tangible form or medium of expression, now known or later developed, from which they can be perceived, reproduced or otherwise communicated, either directly or indirectly with the aid of a machine or device.

CREATIVE WORK: A work is "created" when it is fixed in a copy or phonorecord for the first time. Where a work is created over a period of time, the portion of it that has been fixed constitutes the work as of that time; where the work has been prepared in different versions, each version constitutes a separate work. The source of copyright ownership is the "creator" or author of a work.

A DERIVATIVE WORK is one created from or based on one or more preexisting works. If derived from extensive re-writing, elaboration or adaptation, it is considered to be an original work — such as a motion picture based on a novel.

PHONORECORDS are materials, other than audiovisual materials, in which sounds are fixed by any method now known or later developed, and from which sounds can be perceived, reproduced or otherwise communicated, either directly or with the aid of a machine or device.

COPIES are material objects, other than phonorecords, in which a work is first fixed by any method now known or later developed, and from which the work can be perceived, reproduced or otherwise communicated, either directly or with the aid of a machine or device. "Copies" may refer to originals or duplicate manuscripts, motion pictures, photographs, sculptures, written music and art work.

A CONVENTIONAL sound recording.

SOUND RECORDINGS refer to original and copyrightable works of authorship comprising musical, vocal or other sounds fixed in some tangible form. Such recordings comprise the aggregate of sounds, not the materials in which they are fixed. In this way sound recordings differ from "phonorecords", the latter being the *materials* in which sounds are fixed.

FAIR USE: No acceptable general definition fits the term since it is an evolving judicial doctrine based on an attempt to balance the exclusive rights of creators (authors) against the non-commercial needs of specialized users. (See Chapter Six.)

LITERARY WORKS are works other than audiovisual works; they are expressed in words, numbers or other verbal or numerical symbols or indicia, such as in books, periodicals, manuscripts, photorecords, film, tapes, disks or cards.

AUDIOVISUAL WORKS consist of a series of related images which are intrinsically intended to be shown by the use of machines or devices, together with accompanying sound.

A COLLECTIVE WORK is one, such as a periodical, anthology or encyclopedia, in which separate and independent works are assembled.

A COMPLIATION consists of preexisting materials or data, selected or arranged in such a way that the resulting work constitutes an original work of authorship. The term "compilation" includes collective works.

A PSEUDONYMOUS WORK is one whose author is identified by a fictitious name.

A WORK MADE FOR HIRE is (a) one prepared by an employee within the scope of his or her employment. Or (b) is one prepared as a work of authorship — ordered and executed for a valuable consideration agreed upon in advance. The agreement must be confirmed in writing and clearly state that the work shall be "a work made for hire."

PUBLICATION: A work is "published" if one or more copies or phonorecords embodying it are distributed to the public by lending, rental, lease, sale or other transfer of ownership. The offer to distribute copies or phonorecords to persons for purposes of further distribution, public performance or public display constitutes "publication". A public performance or display does not in itself constitute publication.

FIXATION: A work is considered "fixed" in a tangible medium of expression when its inclusion in a copy or phonorecord — with the author's authority — is sufficiently permanent or stable to permit it to be perceived, reproduced or otherwise communicated for a period of more than transitory duration. A work consisting of sounds, images, or both, that are being transmitted is legally "fixed" if a durable recording of the work is made simultaneously with its transmission.

ORIGINAL WORKS OF AUTHORSHIP characterizes the general subject matter of statutory copyright protection. Two identifying elements — an original work and its tangible form — must merge through fixation to form a product that qualifies for copyright under the Act.

ACT: Signifies the Copyright Act.

A JOINT WORK is one created by two or more authors on the understanding that their respective contributions will be merged into inseparable or interdependent parts of a unified whole.

CHILDREN are a person's immediate offspring, whether legitimate or not, as well as children legally adopted by that person.

TRANSFER OF COPYRIGHT OWNERSHIP is a voluntary assignment, mortgage, exclusive license or any other conveyance, alienation or hypothecation of a copyright or of any of the exclusive rights comprised in a copyright, but not including a non-exclusive license.

DEVICE, MACHINE, PROCESS is one now known or later developed.

DISPLAY: To display a work means to show a copy of it, either directly or by means of film, slide, TV image or any other device or process.

BEST EDITION is the edition of a work published in the United States at any time before the date of deposit, which the Library of Congress deems most suitable for its purpose.

STATES include the 50 states, the District of Columbia, the Commonwealth of Puerto Rico and any territories to which the Copyright Act is made applicable by an Act of Congress.

P.S. Unless you understand copyright terminology you can't understand the law.

Before we consider author-publisher contracts, it is expedient to look at the new Copyright Act which superseded an antiquated act and revised the relationships between authors, industries, institutions and the general public.

The 1976 Copyright Act (Title 17 of the United States Code) covers important legal aspects of many types of creative activity. In copyright terminology *authors* and *authorship* are broad terms applied to the originators of literary, musical, dramatic, graphic, photographic, sculptural and audiovisual works. To keep this exposition within bounds, I shall emphasize the authors who write, especially since books formed the original core around which other works of authorship were added.

After numerous hearings and debates extending over a period of years, many volumes of expert testimony and the vigilance of legal counsel Irwin Karp and other representatives of the Authors League, as well as contributions from many interested organizations, an updated and amended Copyright Act was passed by Congress and signed into law by President Ford on October 19, 1976. Although the new Act took effect on January 1, 1978, it is called the Copyright Act of 1976.

Among the lawmakers who nursed it through a long legislative process, Wisconsin Congressman Robert W. Kastenmeier, Chairman of the House Judiciary Subcommittee responsible for copyrights, distinguished himself for his captaincy of the revision effort. He devoted about 11 years to an analysis and discussion of copyright provisions and to coordinating the views and activities of interested parties. In the upper chamber, the late Arkansas Senator John L. McClellan and Senate colleagues contributed importantly to the formulation and passage of the new Act.

As amended, Title 17 is designed to serve the public interest as well as the numerous individuals, firms, organizations and institutions affected by copyright law. From the standpoint of authors and their rights, the new Act embodies three salient features. They ——

- **provide copyright protection to works of authorship for the author's life plus 50 years**
- **protect, with few exceptions, unpublished works for an author's life plus 50 years**
- **insure that non-dramatic literary works are not subject to compulsory licensing for public broadcasting**

In further explanation of these benefits, all copyrights obtained before January 1, 1978, remain in force for 28 years. However a renewal under the new Act will protect a copyright for another 47 years, giving a two-term protection of 75 years. Thus a work copyrighted in 1966 would be eligible for renewal in 1994. If a renewal registration is made at the proper time, the work will be protected until the year 2041, giving 75 years of continuous coverage. If not, copyright protection terminates at the end of the first (28-year) term.

Coverage for More Than a Century

The maximum copyright protection under the old act was 56 years; but the new Act may protect an author and his heirs for more than a century. For example, if you receive a copyright at age 25 and live to age 80, the copyright remains in force for 105 years. Your heirs or estate would qualify for benefits during the last 50 years.

The second salient provision of the new Act rewards originality and creativity with full Federal copyright protection for fixed but unpublished or unrecorded works, resolving a dilemma that has nagged authors since 1834 when the Supreme Court ruled, as the British House of Lords had ruled in 1774, that unpublished works are protected only by common law. Each of the 50 states has its own common law.

Under the new Act, statutory protection for unpublished works ranges from 75 to 100 years. After publication an author may, of his own volition, register his printed work, especially since it will differ, more or less, from the original manuscript. Also he will be required to deposit two copies of the published book with the Register of Copyrights.

Consider for a moment the plight of Charles Darwin who immersed himself for about 20 years in deep thought over a theory of evolution before committing his ideas to print. Darwin conceived evolution by natural selection and adaptation as early as 1838, carefully recording his ideas in a notebook. About 20 years later he received a letter from the East Indies in which Alfred R. Wallace, a student of plant and animal life, outlined virtually an identical theory of evolution based on his field research.

Avoiding a Serious Conflict

Since Darwin and Wallace were gentlemen as well as scholars, they described their respective theories in essays and submitted them to a jury of scientists. The consensus view, readily accepted by Wallace, credited Darwin with being the originator of evolution by natural selection. His copyrighted book, the classic *Origin of Species,* appeared in 1859.

Such embarassing situations are avoidable now because the new Act affords full copyright protection to unpublished works in a fixed form. Authors and other originators may now feel more secure against misunderstandings or infringements when they circulate unpublished materials to editors, publishers, broadcasters and agents.

The third salient clause in the new Act represents a stunning victory for the Authors League of America. Its spokesmen spearheaded a drive to persuade lawmakers and public (i.e., non-commercial) broadcasters to agree that the negotiation of contractual rights to broadcast non-dramatic literary works is preferable to a system of compulsory licensing.

New Dimensions of Authorship and Copyright

By winning the right under the new law to bargain with broadcasters, writers fixed attention on the expanding scope of authorship and copyright in an era of untold possibilities in communications technology. Nothing like it was imagined about three centuries ago when Queen Anne set her seal on the statute that bears her name, a brave effort to correct the evils and hardships that beset an infant publishing industry.

In Elizabethan time (1558-1603) conditions arising from the advent of printing and publishing were even more dismal. All books considered heretical were burned. A few titles were reprinted several times but the volume of sales did not affect an author's meager income.

Printing, publishing and authorship were hazardous occupations, badgered by legal restraints, decrees, censorship, licensing and literary piracy. Many manuscripts were circulated privately to select readers. To avoid infringements, plays were often kept out of print, but Shakespeare's popular dramas were pirated. Authors were known as people of the "empty purse" and many were sentenced to a debtor's prison. John Milton, sold his masterpiece, *Paradise Lost,* for 18 pounds. Lessor authors were paid in shillings and spare copies of their books. England's publishing operations centered in the city of London.

M. T. CICERO's

CATO MAJOR,

OR HIS

DISCOURSE

OF

OLD-AGE:

With Explanatory NOTES.

PHILADELPHIA:
Printed and Sold by B. FRANKLIN,
MDCCXLIV.

BENJ. FRANKLIN, ESQ.

PIONEER AMERICAN PRINTER AND EXAMPLES OF HIS WORK

FEW MEN can match Franklin's record as a communicator through authorship, printing, diplomacy, statesmanship, science, invention, wit and wisdom. He was also Father of the U.S. Postal System and its first Postmaster General.

A

CATALOGUE

OF

CHOICE AND VALUABLE

BOOKS,

CONSISTING OF

Near 600 Volumes, in moſt Faculties and Sciences, *viz.*

DIVINITY, HISTORY, LAW, MATHEMATICS, PHILOSOPHY, PHYSIC, POETRY, &c.

Which will begin
TO BE SOLD for Ready Money only, by BENJ. FRANKLIN, at the *Poſt-Office* in *Philadelphia*, on Wedneſday, the 11th. of *April* 1744. at Nine a Clock in the Morning; And, for Diſpatch, the loweſt Price is mark'd in each Book.
The Sale to continue Three Weeks, and no longer; and what then remains will be ſold at an advanced Price.

Thoſe Perſons that live remote, by ſending their Orders and Money to ſaid B. FRANKLIN, may depend on the ſame Juſtice as if preſent.

Poor Richard, 1733.

AN

Almanack

For the Year of Chriſt

1733,

Being the Firſt after LEAP YEAR:

And makes ſince the Creation	Years
By the Account of the Eaſtern *Greeks*	7241
By the Latin Church, when ☉ ent. ♈	6932
By the Computation of *W. W.*	5742
By the *Roman* Chronology	5682
By the *Jewiſh* Rabbies	5494

Wherein is contained

The Lunations, Eclipſes, Judgment of the Weather, Spring Tides, Planets Motions & mutual Aſpects, Sun and Moon's Riſing and Setting, Length of Days, Time of High Water, Fairs, Courts, and obſervable Days.

Fitted to the Latitude of Forty Degrees, and a Meridian of Five Hours Weſt from *London*, but may without ſenſible Error ſerve all the adjacent Places, even from *Newfoundland* to *South-Carolina*.

By *RICHARD SAUNDERS*, Philom.

PHILADELPHIA:
Printed and ſold by *B. FRANKLIN*, at the New Printing Office near the Market.

Such were the rude beginnings of the publishing industry as it struggled against heavy odds. By contrast with that industry today, the most appropriate remark is Samuel F. B. Morse's question, "What hath God wrought?" In the first place, Morse himself had brought forth an alphabet of dots and dashes:

THE MORSE DOT-AND-DASH CODE

THE DOT-AND-DASH TELEGRAPHIC CODE invented by Samuel F. B. Morse, the first system of electrical communication, invented in 1836.

Based in part on age-old gestures and signals, an effective international alphabet for deaf persons was perfected by dedicated scholars. The first eight letters of the universal American Sign Language (AMESLAN) are:

THE MANUAL ALPHABET

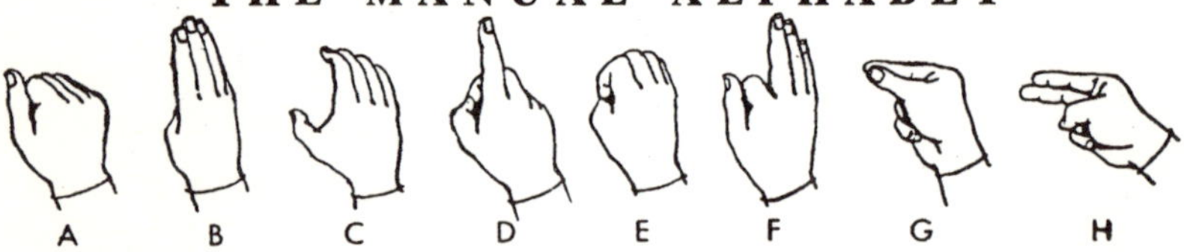

(AS SEEN BY THE SENDER)

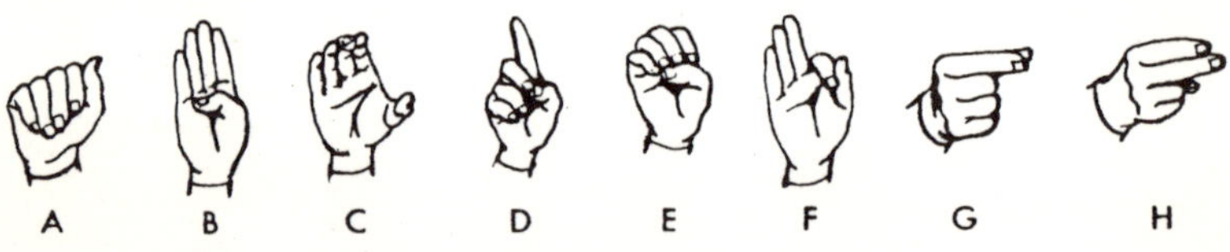

(AS SEEN BY THE RECEIVER)

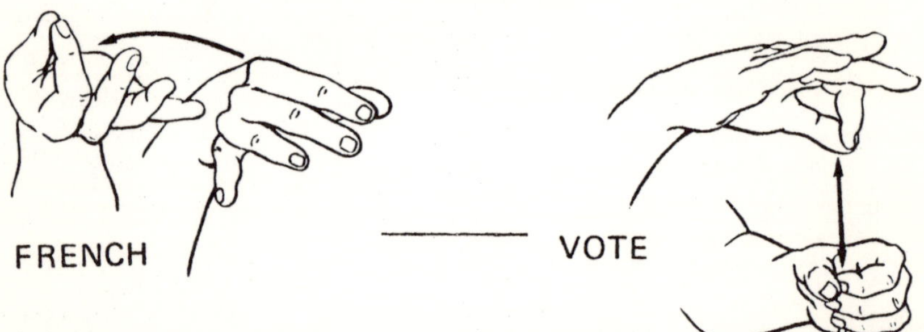

SILENCE SPOKEN HERE

PERSONS BEREFT OF HEARING were once at a loss to communicate, but this handicap was largely overcome by an alphabet of manual speech developed by Juan Pablo Bonet, a 17th century Spaniard.
Almost any word or idea may be spelled out by the silent alphabet which has its own grammatical structure and an adaptability for concrete or abstract expression. With slight modification, the modern American Manual Alphabet has been adopted as the official alphabet by the World Federation of the Deaf.

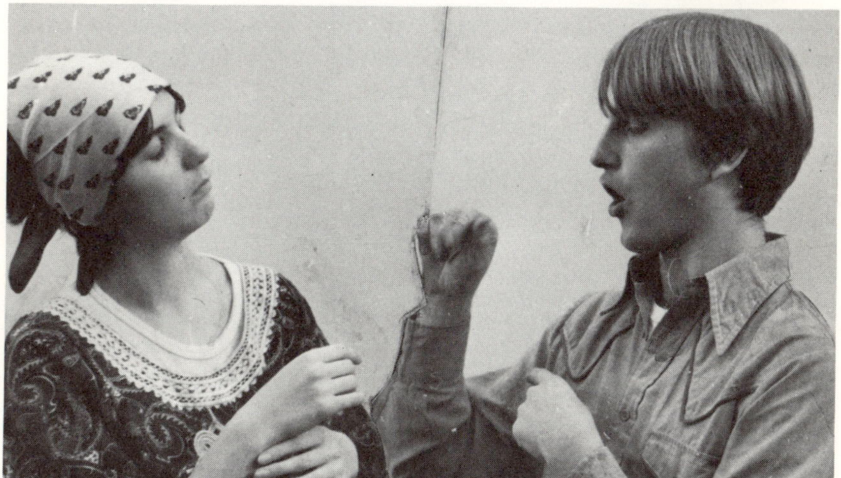

Another silent system of communication, adapted to synthetic dialects like Fortran and Cobol, had its birth early in the 19th century, but is now the centerpiece of a Computer Age. Robot computers make complex computations, solve technical riddles and render statistical decisions.

JACQUARD'S "PUNCH-CARD" LOOM

IBM printout

From Abacus to Copyrights

THE ABACUS, A PRIMITIVE CHINESE CALCULATOR, dates back some 2000 years, that is, to the Year One B.C. (Before Computers) but is still used in some localities.

Many centuries later, in 1804, French engineer Joseph Marie Jacquard, learned to control the operation of a loom with a series of punched cards, a system still used in the textile industry.

The Computer Age was born in 1822 when Charles Babbage, a British thinker, invented a Difference Engine and won a Gold Medal from the Royal Astronomical Society. His machine could generate tables to an accuracy of six decimal places.

Next Babbage drew plans for a steam-powered giant that would take directions from a planned instruction program stored on punch cards. The robot's "brain" was designed with a memory or data storage section for entry data and instructions and an output section for printing results. Since this machine could make mathematical decisions, Babbage named it an Analytical Engine.

The brilliant concept languished for many years. Eventually punched card systems were widely adopted but the great breakthrough came when electromagnetic circuits, as fast as lightning, superseded electro-mechanical circuits.

Today's computers communicate through electronic lingos like Fortran, Cobol and Basic while carrying on superhuman tasks that are essential to the welfare of our society. Tax collecting, population census, social security, monetary controls, stock market trading and the tracking of space vehicles would be practically impossible without computers. Hence they are likely to remain an important part of our daily lives.

The Copyright Office not only uses computers but issues registration certificates for published and unpublished computer programs and printouts. Such data may be protected under the formal provisions of the Copyright Act. A Federal Commission called CONTU is studying possible extensions of copyright coverage in computer technology.

Verily, God hath wrought many things. In the closing years of the 20th century, the dimensions of the revolution induced by technology, authorship and copyrights is staggering. A booming world population and ingenious communications devices have accelerated a global demand for more printed and audible words along with graphics and pictures. Radio and TV networks span oceans and continents; practically the whole of humanity can see or listen to programs broadcast via satellites. Teleprinters, punch-tape machines, photo typesetting and instantaneous transmission of pictures symbolize the new communications technology. Rotary presses disgorge tons of newsprint within an hour. Figuring the daily wordage produced and transmitted by the modern media is an exercise in frustration.

Global communication of sight-and-sound news events, an ancient dream, is now a commonplace. In the last several years, five satellites in synchronous orbits at an altitude of 22,240 miles have linked every corner of the globe in an all-weather communications complex. One satellite has a capacity of two TV channels and 6000 voice channels; by 1980 Intelstat V will double the voice channels. This cosmic communications miracle is a by-product of the original Comsat system.

Torrents of sweet, sour, prophetic, polite, diplomatic and blunt language pours into the communications machinery. Coded, punched, printed, translated and illustrated words facilitate the world's business and cement the building blocks of social order. The creative force

COMMAND STATION at Vernon Valley, N.J. controls communications in RCA's domestic satellite system, providing, voice, video and data services.

behind this conglomerate of words consists of employed and self-employed writers who produce the original texts, giving expression to news events, plans, endeavors, conflicts, hopes, discoveries and fiction. At the same time, they entertain, inform, influence and motivate a far-flung audience. Certainly these wordsmiths are not equally competent or eloquent; neither are they equally paid and rewarded.

The sum of human knowledge and culture is preserved in books, documents, art work and recordings. The originals and copies of such works fill miles and miles of shelving, holding about 75 million items in the Library of Congress alone. Quite a few million items are currently copyrighted and even more millions have passed into the public domain. New registration claims pour into the Copyright Office at the rate of more than 400,000 per year, a fair indication of the mounting volume of copyright material. No monetary value can be assigned to the works protected by copyright and their value doubtless runs into many billions of dollars. With the new legislation authorizing copyrights for unpublished works, registrations are likely to soar.

Another clue to trends in authorship in the United States appears in the mounting figures of book sales, now approaching $5 billion per year, culminating a steady rise over the past decade during which paperbound books registered the largest increase in sales volume. Although about 70 percent of unit sales are paperbacks, sales of hardcover books account for about 65 percent of book industry revenues.

SOPHISTICATED MERCHANDISING along with an unprecedented abundance and variety of new books attract readers of all ages to bookshops.

Satellite Communications

IN THE FONDEST DREAMS OF SCIENTISTS, STATESMEN AND VISIONARIES, no method of communication ever approached the versatility, range and efficiency of man-made satellites. Only a global war or revolution could change the world more rapidly than satellite communication.

So effectively have their signals blanketed the Earth that only a small fraction of its surface remains untouched. Satellites speak any and all languages. They transmit monologues, dialogues, facsimiles, programs, codes, news, intelligence and pictures in a rainbow of colors. And all this within seconds. A total communication system, satellites bind the human family into an intimacy and unity hitherto unknown.

With satellite stations parked at an altitude of 22,240 miles above the Earth, telephone users in more than 250 American cities can now dial their calls directly to 30 countries without operator assistance. In more than 20 countries, people can direct-dial their calls to the United States.

Satellites and computers have something in common: they demand more and more inputs of codes, figures, words and symbols, thus stimulating the communications boom beyond all precedents.

At this writing, there are more than 1000 working satellites, receiving, transmitting and directing multi-lingual traffic in telephony, news, communiqués, data and secret intelligence. Somewhere underground in the Colorado mountains, the North American Air Defense Command maintains a computerized watch on man-made objects in the air spaces above the Earth.

A United States domestic satellite service began with Westar I in April 1974, followed by Westar II, sponsored by Western Union, in October 1974. Now it appears that the era of land-line transmission of network radio and television may be nearing an end. The Mutual Broadcasting System has contracted to service its network of some 870 stations via the Westar satellite system. This will enable Mutual to feed six stereo programs simultaneously, providing a uniform reception quality across the country.

Satellites appear to be equally useful for regional and national publications such as The Wall Street Journal which pioneered the first satellite-transmitted newspaper in 1975. Page-proofs are transmitted from a production plant in Chicopee, Massachusetts, to a printing plant in Orlando, Florida. The Journal's satellite edition has proved eminently successful, foreshadowing a much wider use by periodicals.

The tremendous promise of satellite communication was first realized in 1965 when "Early Bird" began relaying international television programs. Two or three minutes of that satellite's time cost broadcasters several thousand dollars, but the present-day fee is just several hundred dollars. It would require volumes to detail the success stories attributed to satellites. As evidence of progress since "Early Bird", the Washington-based Communications Satellite Corporation (Comsat) manages and services satellite communications for more than 100 countries and territories. Both the satellites and ground equipment in this

TEN-STORY ANTENNA COMPLEX at Etam, West Virginia, shielded against radio interference, transmits at a rate of 50,000 words per minute. It is owned by Comsat, RCA and several other American communications firms.

ARTIST'S SKETCH shows how four synchronized satellites, appropriately stationed, can give saturation coverage to an entire hemisphere.

global system are owned by the International Telecommunications Satellite Organization (Intelsat) whose membership comprises nations with various amounts of investment shares.

Intelsat operates on a profit and loss basis, which Communist China has agreed to abide, but the Soviets are non-signatory users. At the same time, they have established Inter-Sputnik, their own international system, but the only subscribers are east European members of the Communist bloc. Also noteworthy is that the "hot line" between the White House and the Kremlin now depends upon satellites instead of land lines and submarine cables.

In addition to more than 22,000 voice circuits, Intelsat provides its client countries with communication services for telegraph, telex, facsimile, data and television, giving new impetus to the concept of One World.

For satellites there appears to be no end in sight. Just off the drawing board is Intelsat V, 52 feet long, representing a new generation of space communicators. It is capable of handling 12,000 simultaneous two-way telephone conversations and two color television channels. Its wings are covered with thousands of solar cells, converting the sun's energy into 1700 watts of electric power. Weighing two tons at lift-off, it will energize itself by sunpower. When launched in 1979, Intelsat V will expand the present global network considerably.

AT RECEIVING END in Orlando, film negatives are checked for clarity.

3

Four Classes of Works

All Forms of Writing, Speaking, Dancing, Acting and Art Expression Derive from the Human Need to Communicate

ONE OF THE ADMINISTRATIVE BOONS arising from the new Copyright Act is a simplified classification system, reducing the former 15 classes to an all-embracing four classes. A fifth class, called RE, will eventually pass out of existence since it applies only to renewals for works originally copyrighted between January 1, 1950 and December 31, 1977.

Even a cursory review makes it apparent that the range and scope of original works eligible for copyright encompasses virtually every creative activity. But new technology involving computers, space exploration and laser beams will doubtless open new fields for copyright.

Any copyrightable work registered after January 1, 1978, naturally falls into one of the following classes:

CLASS TX, NONDRAMATIC LITERARY WORKS: Save for dramatic works and certain types of audiovisual works, Class TX covers both published and unpublished works written in verbal or numerical computer symbols. TX includes works of fiction and nonfiction, periodicals, poetry, textbooks, references, catalogs, advertising copy and compilations of information. A more detailed treatment of literary works appears in later chapters. The computer uses of copyrighted works are under close study. Sooner or later, the emerging patterns of computer technology will enable lawmakers to formulate appropriate legislation.

CLASS PA, WORKS OF THE PERFORMING ARTS: This class covers published and unpublished works capable of being performed before a live audience, or indirectly "by means of any device or process." Class PA covers musical works and accompanying music; pantomimes and choreographic works; motion pictures and other audiovisual works.

In copyright terminology a musical composition is a work of original authorship consisting of music alone or of words and music combined.

LEONARD BERNSTEIN, COMPOSER,
conducts with a strong presence
and sensitive baton.

A song poem or lyric alone does not qualify as a musical composition.

In filing for copyright protection, the author-composer submits his claim with a legible musical notation; lyrics should preferably be written under the notes. A complete version of the work, published or unpublished, should accompany the claim to registration. A tape recording or other type of recorded sound is acceptable as a depository copy.

The Copyright Office does not "grant" or "issue" copyrights; it registers claims to copyrights and issues Certificates of Registration. The author-composer obtains a Certificate by registering an original work in published or unpublished form.

The approved methods of copyrighting a musical composition are: by registering it in the Copyright Office in unpublished form; or by publishing the composition with a statutory copyright notice affixed to each copy.

Publication of a musical work means the public distribution or sale of copies. It is advisable to affix copyright notices to all copies circulating among music professionals or offered for public sale.

It is also advisable to register a copyright claim promptly after publication. Obtain and fill out Application Form PA, send it along with two complete copies of the composition and a $10 fee to the Register of Copyrights, Washington, D.C. 20559.

On sheet music the copyright notice should be placed on the title page or first page of music. About 60 countries, including the United States, adhere to the Universal Copyright Convention (UCC). A published work of sheet music composed by a United States citizen may obtain protection in member countries of UCC by affixing a copyright notice to each copy, thus:

© 1978 by John Doe

ARTUR RUBINSTEIN at the piano. His original interpretations and arrangements of classic works are copyrightable.

The Pan American Copyright Convention provides reciprocal protection in most of the American republics.

The owner of a copyrighted musical composition enjoys the exclusive right to make new arrangements of his work and to perform it publicly for a profit.

After the owner makes a sound recording of his work or authorizes others to do it, anyone may choose one of two options for recording that same work:

- **he may obtain a legal compulsory license, that is, a license without the owner's consent; however, the licensee is legally obligated to pay the owner fixed royalty fees**
- **he may negotiate and sign a sound recording contract with the copyright owner**

A person who records copyrighted music under a compulsory license is required to give advance notice. He should send a Notice of Intention to Use to the copyright owner by registered mail and forward a duplicate copy of such notice, which does not require a standardized printed form, to the Copyright Office. A $6 fee covers one to five musical compositions named together.

Works in Choreography

This art may be defined as the craft of "writing" or designing dances. In copyright terminology a choreographic work is a ballet or similar theatrical work that relates a story and develops a character or ex-

CHOREOGRAPHER GEORGE BALANCHINE, maestro of the ballet, instructing a ballerina.

presses an emotional theme by means of well-defined dance movements and actions. Hence it relates both to drama and the art of interpretive motion.

"Choreography" is not mentioned in the Copyright Act, but this dance art is copyrightable because Class PA covers dramatic or dramatico-musical compositions. To qualify for registration, a work must meet two requirements:

First, the dance action must convey a dramatic concept or idea and be sufficient in itself for performance without further additions.

Second, the movements and actions of the dance must be fixed and recorded in a legibly-written or illustrated form, providing detailed descriptions, notations, pictures or diagrams or both. Film strips or motion picture sequences of the dance may also be submitted with the claim to registration.

A copyrighted work protects only the choreographic style and expression of movements as conceived and fixed by the author. However, a copyright does not protect the work's idea or theme. Additionally, social, ballroom and folk dances are not considered copyrightable material.

To register an unpublished choreographic work, the claimant should request and fill out an application on Form PA and attach a complete copy of the acting form of the work. If this copy is just a diagram of dance movements, it should be supplemented by a description of the work as a whole, including the plot, characters, theme and staging.

To register a published work, the author is required to submit two copies of the choreographic manuscript with the copyright notice. In the copyright sense, "publication" of a work usually means that copies of the manuscript have been distributed or offered for sale. The per-

SCULPTOR Alfredo Halegua in his Washington atelier.

formance of a choreographic work is not considered a qualification for "publication".

CLASS VA, WORKS OF THE VISUAL ARTS: Certain two and three-dimensional works of fine, graphic and applied art, including photographs, prints, art reproductions, maps, globes, technical drawings, diagrams and models may be protected by the Copyright Act.

Included are works of artistic craftsmanship insofar as their form but not their mechanical or utilitarian aspects are concerned. In this category, the design of a useful article may be considered a copyrightable work only if, and only to the extent that, such design incorporates pictorial, graphic or sculptural features that can be identified separately from, and are capable of existing independently of, the utilitarian aspects.

Benefits to Copyright Owners

The extended duration of copyright and other benefits of the new Act apply to original works of art and craftsmanship as well as to works of literature and music.

The owner's exclusive right to reproduce a pictorial, graphic or sculptural work includes the right to reproduce the work in or on any kind of article, whether useful or not. Owners also have the right to display or authorize others to display their pictorial, graphic or sculptured works publicly. But a copyright does not exclude others from making, distributing or displaying pictures or photos of such articles in connection with advertisements or commentaries related to the distribution or display of such articles, or in connection with news re-

GRAPHIC ARTIST John Pack in his studio workshop.

ports.

Following a Supreme Court ruling in 1954, a copyrighted pictorial, graphic or sculptured work will not be adversely affected if the work is employed in the design of a useful article; and it will afford protection to the copyright owner against an unauthorized reproduction of his work.

An owner may reproduce, adapt, publish and display his work. However if an artisan or craftsman creates and produces a work "within the scope of his employment" by a firm or individual for a salary or a fee, he is considered an "employee for hire" and hence ineligible to file a copyright registration claim. Only his employer can file such a claim.

Works in the category of visual arts, both published and unpublished, may be copyrighted as soon as they are in a tangible or fixed form. In copyright terminology, a work is "published" when copies are placed on sale or publicly distributed. An unrestricted public exhibition of a work may also constitute "publication."

Copyrighting Maps

Maps of geographic areas, including relief maps or models, road maps, street maps, celestial maps, atlases, global maps and marine charts may be copyrighted. But outline maps are generally ineligible because they lack originality in form or content.

Where a substantial part of a map is based on previously published sources, a statement of what was added or revised should be written on the registration claim. A map published without the required notice does not invalidate the copyright, provided that "a reasonale effort is made" to add the notice after the omission is discovered.

RECORDINGS of original music and speeches may be deposited with claims for registration.

Models and Designs for Works of Art

This group takes in published or unpublished pictorial, graphic or sculptured works, comprising original paintings, drawings, etchings, engravings, sculptures, carvings in relief and other works identified with the arts. It also includes works embodied in, superimposed on or applied to useful articles, such as jewelry, enamel, glassware and textiles. The works may be abstract or representational. However, regardless of form, no work is entitled to statutory protection unless it can be considered the "original writing of an author" within the meaning of the Copyright Act.

What Is Copyrightable and What Is Not

To receive a copyright a work of art must contain an appreciable amount of original pictorial, graphic or sculptural material. If not, a copyright registration will be withheld. However, a work's artistic merit and aesthetic appearance are not evaluated by a copyright examiner. Expressions of originality and creativity are the prime considerations.

Various works of art may be embodied in utilitarian, ornamental or aesthetic forms. But an author's plan or reason for creating such a work has no bearing on its acceptance for registration. Certain original works may be eligible for a copyright as well as for a patent under the design patent law, administered by the Commissioner of Patents and Trademarks, Washington, D.C. 20231.

Artists and craftsmen should be aware that neither the titles of their works nor ideas expressed or reflected in them are copyrightable. Titles and ideas have no legal right to copyright exclusivity. Also a utilitarian work lacking original artistic features such as sculpture, carving or pictorial representation, worthy of existing independently as art or craftsman ship, cannot be copyrighted.

Two or more unpublished art works may be registered as a "collection", with a single application and copyright fee, provided that the collection—

PHOTOGRAPHING art works in the National Gallery, Washington.

- **is assembled in an orderly form**
- **bears a single-line title**
- **is the subject of a single copyright claim**
- **represents the work of a single author**

An unpublished work may be registered by completing Form VA, provided by the Copyright Office, and by depositing a copy or an identifying reproduction of the work along with the required fee. Two copies are required when registering a published work. The copyright notice, with or without a date, must be permanenty affixed to an accessible portion of the work.

Reproduction of Art Works

Copyrighted reproductions of original works of art may be made by the owner or authorized by him. Such reproductions may be made on textile, metal, paper or in three-dimensional forms. Registration claims should be filed on Form VA.

Drawings Or Plastic Works of a Technical Nature

The term "plastic" refers to the sculptured or molded forms of three-dimensional works, not to the materials of which they are made.

To be eligible for copyright, a drawing must contain an appreciable amount of original graphic or pictorial matter; and a plastic work must embody an appreciable amount of original sculptural material.

In this group, or any other group of work, it is not possible to copyright ideas, plans, methods, systems, procedures or programs. Neither can you copyright forms, devices or articles designed for computing, measuring or recording, since they lack "creative authorship."

Copyrighting Photographs

This group covers "still" photographic prints, film strips, slide films and individual slides, in color or in black-and-white. But not all

THE CAMERA'S EYE captures and communicates a picture taken in one fleeting moment.

photographs are copyrightable; they must express an appreciable amount of originality of a pictorial nature.

Both published and unpublished photographs may be copyrighted. The notice may consist of the symbol © accompanied by initials or an appropriate mark, provided that the owner's name appears in some permanently accessible portion of the work.

Prints and Pictorial Illustrations

This category comprises illustrations, greeting cards, picture postcards, posters, placemats and similar prints produced by lithography, rotogravure, photoengraving or other methods. A print or label containing copyrightable pictorial matter or text, or both, published in connection with the sale or advertisement of an article of mechandise, may also be registered. As with other art works, pictorial illustrations and prints must offer an appreciable amount of original graphic or pictorial craftsmanship in order to be copyrighted.

CLASS SR, SOUND RECORDINGS: This category is appropriate for published and unpublished works in which (1) the copyright claim is limited just to the audible sound recording itself and (2) in which the same copyright claimant seeks a registration which covers, in addition to the sound recording, the music composition as well as a dramatic or literary work embodied in the recording.

With one exception, Class SR recordings consist of a fixed combination of musical, vocal or other sounds. The exception applies to sound recordings harmoniously and compatibly attached to audiovisual works, such as the soundtracks of motion pictures or audio cassettes accompanying film strips. As integral parts of audiovisual works, such recordings are registrable in Class PA, the performing arts. Sound recordings fixed before February 15, 1972, are not eligible for Federal registration but may be protected under State law.

4

Your Life Plus Fifty Years

Like Genesis, Copyright Begins with an Act of Original Creation; by Itself, This Act Is the Cornerstone of Copyright Law

IN A FAR-REACHING IMPROVEMENT, the new Copyright Act established a single-term system, susperseding the archaic dual system which we inherited from the early 18th century. A copyright for a work in fixed form may endure for the life of the author and 50 years beyond.

The antiquated two-term system offered a maximum protection for 56 years. In 1909, when the previous major copyright revision was enacted, life expectancy in America also amounted to about 56 years; but in the 1970's a person's life expectancy exceeded 70 years, fully justifying an extended copyright term. A short term discriminates against many serious creative works whose value may not appear until many years have elapsed. Moreover the rapid development of communications media has broadened and extended the commercial life of some works.

The basic provision of the new Act — called its "foundation" — is an uninterrupted lifetime of protection, after which copyright benefits inure to the author's heirs or assigns. Even so, the whole term of a copyright is not fixed; it may on occasion continue beyond one century, with no fear of expiration or need for renewal. In return for the "life plus 50" clause, authors have given up their perpetual and exclusive common law rights in unpublished works. A large majority of foreign countries have adopted "life plus 50" terms of copyright. West Germany provides life plus 70 years.

Where two or more persons collaborate in creating a copyrightable work, they share the rights and benefits. The new Act provides that the length of copyright protection will extend 50 years beyond the death of the last surviving collaborator.

"Life plus 50" offers one of the strongest inducements to creative authorship in the history of the American copyright system. Moreover the "author" — whether he or she is a writer, composer, sculptor,

UNDER PRESENT LAW an original manuscript in a fixed form is eligible for copyright protection immediately after its creation.

photographer, artist or choreographer — receives an added incentive in the form of Federal statutory protection for unpublished original works, that is, works that have not been duplicated, sold or distributed publicly.

A work is eligible for copyright protection from the first day of its creation if it is original, tangible and "fixed". In other words, it must not bear a close resemblance to any other work; it must also be a completed work and "fixed" in a tangible, visible or audible form. It may be revised or amended after creation; if so, each revision or version consttiutes a new work.

Under the law, an original symphony, sculpture, photograph, dictionary, catalog, painting or novel may satisfy the statutory criteria for a copyright. All are considered to be works of "authorship".

The various authorial works fall into three groups:

- **works published during an author's lifetime**
- **works published posthumously**
- **unpublished works in fixed form**

Under the old Act an unpublished book manuscript could not be copyrighted under Federal law; it was protected by the common laws of the 50 respective states. The odd thing about the old common law was a provision for "perpetual protection." The present Federal law has abrogated that concept and inaugurated profound changes by restricting the copyright jurisdiction of State common laws. The old concept of "publication" as a condition for copyrighting a book has lost its importance as a dividing line between a State's common law and Federal statutory protection. In effect, the new Act abolishes any right or protection under common law that falls within the scope of Federal copyright law.

Before 1978 the State laws provided perpetual protection for unpublished works. Present Federal law forbids the perpetual protection of fixed works and all such laws have been scrapped.

The States are, however, still involved in the security of original works, since Federal law sanctions common law protection for works that are not fixed in a tangible form or medium of expression. In this way State laws cover, for instance, choreography that has never been filmed or notated, extemporaneous speeches not recorded, or unwritten music that has not been recorded.

Such works may be said to exist, although under Federal law they have not yet been "created". The various State laws protect them up to the point of "fixation", after which they qualify for Federal copyright.

Before reaching "fixation" or "creation" in a copy or sound recording, a work protected by State law subsists in a sort of twilight zone. In its interpretive report on the new Copyright Act, the House Committee on the Judiciary states that up to the point of creation, a work "is subject to common law protection, even though it may exist in someone's mind and may have been communicated to others in unfixed form."

Lending legal protection to something that "may exist in someone's mind" opens a Pandora's Box of revelations that defy imagination.

THE END OF PERPETUAL COPYRIGHTS

WHATEVER COPYRIGHT LAW THE CONGRESS ENACTS must limit the duration of the exclusive rights it secures. All works of authorship must eventually fall into the public domain. We are without power to vest these rights in an author in perpetuity. Whereas common law rights are unlimited as to time, the common law must yield to statutory law wherever statutory law is applicable. So the common law with rights of unlimited duration is displaced by the Congressional law of termination.

—Congressman Edward Hutchinson from Michigan, Member of the Copyright Subcommittee, House Committee on the Judiciary

---

THE LIBRARY OF CONGRESS

EMBRACES the Copyright Office, National Television and Radio Archives, photographic, literary, art, linguistic and musical treasures. The Library catalogs items in 468 languages and employs a staff competent in 120 living languages. The combined collections add up to an impressive 74 million items.

BELOW: An exterior view of Library and bookstacks.

THE GREAT HALL OF THE LIBRARY

HEROIC LIFE-SIZE SCULPTURE FOUNTAIN

5

Your Bundle of Rights

Copyright Is an Author's Economic Lifeline and Legal Shield — the Right from Which All Other Rights Flow

THE NEW ACT emphasizes that the initial copyright of a work is vested in the author. The authors of a joint work are co-owners and considered to be "tenants-in-common", each having the right to use or license a work, subject to an obligation to account to the others for all profits.

In broad terms each copyright endows its owner or owners with five fundamental powers comprising a "bundle", granting exclusive rights to —

- **reproduce**
- **adapt**
- **publish**
- **perform**
- **display**

These rights enable copyright owners to do themselves or to authorize others to do what is expressed or implied. The "bundle" itself is cumulative and its components may overlap. Any of the major rights in the "bundle" may be subdivided, licensed or sold. Each subdivision of an exclusive right may be owned and enforced separately. The owner's right "to authorize" places emphasis on the liability of contributory infringers. To wit, a person who acquires an authorized copy of a motion picture lawfully would be an infringer if he rents it for an unauthorized public performance.

Every copyright establishes an owner's basic right to reproduce, adapt and publish his work. The multiple rights contained in these three categories are related but still independent. A single infringement may violate some or all the rights simultaneously, as where a publisher reproduces, adapts and sells copies of a person's copyrighted work.

The Right to Reproduce or Copy

Whether in copies or sound recordings, the right to reproduce carries with it the right to make or purchase the material in which the work is fixed.

A copyrighted work is infringed either by reproducing it entirely or in some substantial part. Wide departures or variations from the original work would still be an infringement if an author's "expression" rather than his ideas are appropriated. In the context of Federal law, the basic dichotomy between an idea and the author's form or individual style of expressing that idea remains unchanged.

The Right to Adapt for a Derivative Work

The right to adapt a copyrighted work in order to produce a derivative work overlaps the right of reproduction, more or less, since adaptation is a broader undertaking than just reproducing a fixed work. A derivative work may require recasting, re-writing or adapting one or more preexisting works.

To be considered an infringement, a derivative or adapted work must be based on a copyrighted work, resulting in a translation, musical arrangement, dramatization, fictionalization, audio-visualization, sound recording, art reproduction, abridgment, condensation or any other form in which a work may be recast or adapted. In a clearcut violation, the infringing work incorporates a portion of the copyrighted work in some form.

The Right to Publish or Distribute

An owner's exclusive right to distribute copyrighted copies or sound recordings through sales or other transfers of ownership or by rental, lease or lending, includes an authority to control the first public distribution of his work. Any unauthorized first sale or first public distribution of copies or sound recordings would constitute an infringement. An author's exclusive right to sell or display a copy or sound recording of his work ceases after he has made an initial distribution.

Rights of Public Performance

Exclusive public performance rights of an author's works extend to literary, musical, dramatic and choreographic treatments; also to pantomimes, motion pictures and other audiovisual works and recordings.

Rights of Public Display

The new Act contains the first statutory recognition of an author's exclusive right to make public exhibits of a wide range of literary, musical, dramatic, pictorial, graphic or sculptural works. An author's right to display works publicly also covers his right to produce and transmit original, live or recorded performances. However the extent of these rights is not sharply defined.

Transfers of Exclusive Rights or Parts Thereof

Although an author's United States copyright cannot be taken away by an involuntary transfer, except by operation of law, a copyright owner may transfer all his exclusive rights or any subdivision of those rights. A copyright may also be willed as personal property or pass by the applicable laws of intestate succession.

A transfer may consist of an assignment, mortgage, license or any other conveyance, alienation or hypothecation of a copyright or any of its exclusive rights; however non-exclusive licenses cannot be transferred.

A notarized acknowledgment is not required to validate a transfer but is highly desirable. It is also advisable to record transfers and other documents with the actual signatures of the principals and certificating officials. For a filing fee the Register of Copyrights will issue a certificate of recordation. The law forbids infringement claims or suits before the transfer instruments are recorded in the Copyright Office.

A transfer of copyright ownership or any of its rights does not include property rights in material objects; nor, in the absence of a written agreement, does it include the copy or phonorecord in which a work was first fixed.

Termination of Transfers Granted After January 1, 1978

Any long-term transfers of titles, exclusive rights or copyright licenses executed by an author after January 1, 1978 are subject to termination by the author or his beneficial heirs. The only exceptions are works made for hire or works transferred through an author's will.

The new Act provides that all licenses or grants revert to the author or his heirs during a five-year period beginning at the end of 35 years from the date of publication of a work under grant or at the end of 40 years from the date of execution of the grant, whichever comes soonest.

Such a termination is legal regardless of any previous agreement to the contrary. It takes effect after the author or his beneficial heirs serve a written notice on the licensees not less than two or more than ten years before the effective expiration date. Copies of such notices must be recorded in the Copyright Office.

Termination of Works Copyrighted Before the End of 1977

The new Act makes special provisions regarding works in their first or second term of copyright under the old Act, which expired at the end of 1977. Their combined terms of protection were increased from 56 to 75 years.

A Single Registration for Collective Copyrights

Under the old Act it was necessary to pay a fee and to file a registration claim for each copyrighted item. The new Act authorizes an author to pay a single fee to obtain a collective copyright for all stories, articles and other copyrightable materials contributed to various media within a 12-month period.

Copyrights for contributions to collective works, such as anthologies and periodicals, are distinctive and rest initially in the authors of the contributions. The owner of a collective work is presumed to have acquired only the privilege of producing and distributing the several contributions as parts of that collective work, as well as revisions of it.

THE AUTHOR'S BILL OF RIGHTS UNDER THE NEW COPYRIGHT ACT

"THE SOURCE OF COPYRIGHT is the author of the work . . . Copyright vests initially in the author or authors. . . .

"THE UNITED STATES COPYRIGHT of an individual author shall be secured to that author and cannot be taken away by an involuntary transfer.

". . . NO ACTION by any governmental body or other official or organization purporting to seize, expropriate, transfer or exercise rights of ownership with respect to the copyright, or any of the exclusive rights under a copyright, shall be given effect under this title."

(from Section 201, Title 17 of the U.S. Code)

AN AUTHOR'S EXCLUSIVE COPYRIGHT of an original work begins on the day of its creation.

AN AUTHOR CAN DIVIDE and subdivide his copyright and license to lease, lend, grant or bequeath the rights individually or collectively.

A COPYRIGHT REGISTRATION must identify the author of a work. If the claimant is not the author, he must state how he acquired the right to register. A false allegation that the author "was an employee for hire" is a violation of the Act.

THE AUTHOR OF A CONTRIBUTION to a periodical, anthology, symposium or other collective work is, "as in every other case, the first owner of a copyright in it." Unless an author signs a written transfer of rights, he retains ownership of the copyright in his contribution. The transfer of an original copy or phonorecord does not affect ownership in any way.

ANY TRANSFER OF A COPYRIGHT or its subsidiary rights by an author must be voluntary and without coercion or covert pressure.

AUTHOR, YOU CAN —

COPYRIGHT original, unpublished manuscripts or audible, audio-visual or artistic creations in a fixed form.

ENJOY exclusive ownership of a copyright for your lifetime and will it to your heirs or other beneficiaries for 50 years after your death.

RESERVE TO YOURSELF the right to sell, license, transfer, assign or lease your copyrighted work for royalties or other considerations.

REPRODUCE, adapt, publish, broadcast, translate or exhibit your copyrighted work or authorize others to do it for you under negotiated terms.

SAFEGUARD the style, phraseology and distinctive or original way of expressing yourself, whether in fixed literary or art works, music composition, recordings and motion pictures.

AVAIL YOURSELF of legal remedies for infringements of exclusive rights in a registered copyright.

FOR A SINGLE FEE, register your claim for a collective copyright to cover all original contributions to periodicals and newspapers during a 12-month period.

TERMINATE, or your heirs can terminate, a license, lease or grant 35 years after publication date of a work or 40 years after date of a grant, whichever term ends first.

YOU CANNOT —

COPYRIGHT a work in the public domain.

COPYRIGHT the title of a book, play, film or any other original work.

COPYRIGHT ideas, facts, information, discoveries, processes, intangible or unfixed improvisations. Also excluded from copyright are pseudonyms, slogans, expressions, mottoes, catchwords, names of products, organizations and groups. Neither can you preclude others from adapting facts, information and ideas to a different style of expression or choice of diction.

TRANSFER copyright ownership or yield any exclusive rights unless the owner or his authorized agent signs an instrument of conveyance. A notary's seal and signature on this document are not obligatory, but advisable.

ENFORCE your rights in the courts against infringements unless, by registration, you have made a public record of your copyright claim.

6

The Doctrine of "Fair Use"

THUS FAR WE HAVE DWELT ON THE EXCLUSIVITY AND BROAD SWEEP OF RIGHTS granted to copyright owners. There is another side to this coin because the law makes some exceptions to the concept of total exclusivity. For the first time, the 1976 Act gives statutory recognition to various well-established limitations on authorial rights.

Under the protective umbrella of "fair use", these exceptions and limitations have made some inroads on exclusivity. Concerned authors and publishers have protested the proliferation of copying machines and devices in printing plants, offices and libraries on the ground that they injure the sales of copyrighted materials.

In numerous actions, the defendants have claimed that their reproduction of copyrighted works constituted "fair use", not infringements. A number of court decisions have upheld "fair use" as an equitable rule of reason which can be applied as a doctrine of eqüity and fairness.

Notwithstanding the safeguards for copyright exclusivity, a single reproduction of a copy or sound recording for scholarly research, criticism, comment, newsreporting and teaching (with multiple copies for classrooms) is sanctioned by law and does not constitute an infringement.

In determining, on a case-by-case basis, whether the use of any copyrighted work is "fair", the courts have applied such criteria as —

- **THE PURPOSE and character of the use, including whether it is commercial or for non-profit educational purposes**
- **THE NATURE of the copyrighted work**
- **THE AMOUNT and substantiality of the portion used in relation to the copyrighted work as a whole and**
- **THE EFFECT of the use upon the potential market or value of the copyrighted work**

The above criteria for judging alleged infringemnts arose from numerous suits and controversies, mostly involving the reproduction of copyrighted materials for educational and scholarly purposes. While endorsing the principle of "fair use", the new Act does not give it unrestricted support since the courts must remain free to interpret the doctrine in the accordance with rapid technological changes and the individual merits of each case.

"Systematic" Copying Outlawed

Within the scope of regulations, employees of libraries and archives may reproduce a single copy of a work but not for commercial advantage. The Act expressly forbids the "systematic" reproduction of copyrighted works, wherein whole chapters or significant portions are copied. A Copyright Clearance Center has been established as the agency for collecting royalties for photocopying library materials. The proceeds are disbursed to the respective copyright owners.

Stringent regulations recently issued by the Copyright Office relate to the photocopying equipment installed in many libraries for the use of readers. However Section 109 of the new Act authorizes the owner of a single copy or sound recording to sell or otherwise dispose of it "without the authority of the copyright owner."

A teacher in a non-profit educational institution may make single copies of copyrighted matter in connection with scholarly research or classroom preparation. The Act also authorizes the production of multiple copies of certain works but not to exceed one copy per pupil. Also permissable is a performance or display of copyrighted work in the course of face-to-face instruction in a non-profit educational institution. "Fair use" also sanctions performances of nondramatic literary or musical works at religious assemblies or places of worship.

Here are random examples of court decisions in favor of "fair use" on the basis of given circumstances:

- **QUOTATIONS OF EXCERPTS in critical reviews for the purpose of comment or illustration**
- **BRIEF QUOTATIONS from a scholarly or technical work, to illustrate or characterize an author's opinions or observations**
- **USE IN PARODY of some of the contents of the work parodied**
- **SUMMARIES OF AN ADDRESS or article with brief quotations in a news report**
- **REPRODUCTION BY A TEACHER or student of a small part of a work to illustrate a lesson**

REPRODUCTION OF A WORK in judicial proceedings.

OUR ATTEMPTS TO MODERNIZE THE LAW began in 1924. Before World War II revision bills twice passed one house of Congress only to be stymied in the other. The efforts which resulted in the 1976 Copyright Act began in August 1955 when Congress authorized what was to become a six-year study of needed revisions by a special committee under the supervision of the Register of Copyrights.

—Wisconsin Congressman Robert W. Kastenmeier, Chairman of the House Judiciary Subcommittee

7

Licensing Under the New Act

THE NEW ACT embodies both compulsory and non-compulsory licenses. In order to monitor the compliance of owners and users of copyrighted works and to balance fair value against fair compensation, Congress established a five-member Copyright Royalty Tribunal, appointed by the President with the advice and approval of the Senate. The members will serve five to seven years and rotate the chairmanship.

Like the Copyright Office, the Tribunal is directly responsible to Congress; both agencies submit annual reports to the House and Senate. Rulings and decisions of the Tribunal are published in the Federal Register.

The Tribunal's main responsibilities are to determine and adjust copyright royalty rates for certain groups of users; to maximize the availability of creative works to the public; to assure the copyright owner a fair return for his work and the copyright user a fair income for his services.

Four Categories of Compulsory Licenses

The new copyright Act alleviates the loss of control and inadequate compensation formerly received by music composers for the use of their works.

While continuing the compulsory licenses and fees for duplicating and exploiting music recordings, the 1976 Act added three new categories for compulsory licensing — jukeboxes, cable TV and non-commercial public broadcasting. Thus the owners of copyrighted music are now receiving royalties from three user categories which paid nothing before 1978.

The addition of compulsory licenses for three new sources of royalty for copyright owners constitutes a digression which lawmakers justify by pointing to the years of free use enjoyed by various industries. The endless repetition of musical numbers by jukeboxes, non-commercial broadcasting and cable TV will yield cumulative royalties to the owners. Each jukebox is registered and licensed for an annual fee of $8.00, payable to Copyright Office and disbursed by the Royalty Tribunal

LICENSE FEES are levied on coin-operated juke boxes by the Government.

among copyright owners.

Licenses for Non-dramatic Musical Works

Compulsory licenses for phonorecordings of nondramatic musical works have been issued for many years. After an initial distribution by a copyright owner, other persons may obtain a compulsory license to make and distribute sound recordings of the same work, but only if the primary purpose is to distribute and sell to the public for private use. The copyright owner receives royalties on such sales.

Concerts and other public musical events may be somewhat restricted because several organizations representing composers, music publishers and performers are making a determined effort to require organizers and sponsors of such events to obtain licenses in advance of performances, that is, where there is a direct or indirect admissions fee or where compensation is paid to the performers, promoters or organizers. Performance right license fees are payable for all music not in the public domain. Classical compositions which have received new arrangements by modern composers are also subject to license fees.

Non-Compulsory Licenses for Nondramatic Literary Works

These works escaped being the fifth category subject to compulsory licenses because the Authors League mobilized strong resistance to an amendment that would have granted the Public Broadcasting System unlimited access to copyrighted nondramatic literary works — and

THE NEW COPYRIGHT LAW has augmented the incomes of composers.

that without the consent of the authors. The League contended that compulsory licensing would create a dangerous precedent. Leading performance rights societies and book publishers supported the League's position and the amendment was defeated. Consequently the new Act authorizes a voluntary system, providing royalty payments arrived at through negotiation between public broadcasters and copyright owners.

Now that we have a Copyright Royalty Tribunal to regulate, adjudicate and compensate certain parties, some observers wonder whether it marks just a moderate effort to harmonize the relationships of owners and users or the beginning of a trend toward a broad application of compulsory licensing. In this connection the comment of Copyright Register Barbara Ringer is apropos: "In many ways," she said, "the Tribunal is a sensible and ingenious device for making the various compulsory license schemes work efficiently and without constant and unwarranted litigation and need for Congressional action.

"At the same time, the existence of a government body that is paying out royalties, settling disputes, reviewing royalty rates and deciding the terms and rates of licenses, seems an open invitation to further government control. All this bears close watching in the months and years to come."

VIRTUALLY ALL PERFORMANCES and recordings of copyrighted theatrical and musical works are subject to licenses, fees or royalties. Photo above: Scene from an Arena Theater production of a Gorki play. Below: Boston Symphony Orchestra and chorus in an opera recording session.

8

Copyright Infringements

SEVERE PUNISHMENTS for deliberate and wilful copyright infringements are written into the Copyright Act. On numerous occasions the courts have meted out punishment to convicted violators of the criminal provisions of copyright laws.

Infringers are described as persons who violate any of the exclusive rights of the copyright owner or who import copies or recordings into the United States without the copyright owner's authority. The owner is entitled to file an action for damages or losses and other appropriate remedies.

One remedy which the courts apply in a civil action is to serve temporary or final injunctions to restrain or prevent a copyright infringement anywhere in the United States. The court may also order the impounding of copies, phonorecords and equipment which had been used in an infringement. As part of a final decree, the court may order the destruction or other disposal of all materials and equipment made or used in violating a copyright owner's exclusive rights.

Any person found guilty of infringement is liable for the copyright owner's actual damages and any additional profits made by the infringer, as well as for statutory damages.

At any time before final judgment in a court action, a copyright owner may elect to recover, instead of actual damages, an award of statutory damages for all infringements, in a sum not less than $250 or more than $10,000, as the court determines.

Damages for Wilful Infringements

Where the copyright owner proves and the court confirms that the infringement was wilful, the court may increase the award for damages up to $50,000. But where the court finds that the infringer was unaware he was committing a violation, the court may reduce the damages to not less than $100.

In any civil suit the court may allow the recovery of all costs. The court may also award a reasonable attorney's fee to the prevailing party.

Wilful and purposeful infringements of copyright in order to obtain a commercial advantage or private financial gain are subject to fines up to $10,000 and up to a year in prison, or both.

For violations of copyrights in sound recordings and motion pictures, infringers are liable to fines up to $25,000 and up to one year in prison, or both, for the first such offense, with double penalties for any subsequent violations. In addition to cash penalties, the court may order the forfeiture and destruction of all materials and equipment involved in the infringement.

Any person who with fraudulent intent places a notice of copyright on an article or who fraudulently alters or removes a copyright notice or who falsifies material facts in a Copyright Office application, claim or other statement is liable to a fine up to $2500.

All copies or phonorecords, materials and equipment involved in copyright infringements may be seized and forfeited to the United States Government. Finally, all civil and criminal actions involving copyrights must be commenced within three years after the cause of an action occurs.

IS IT SELF-INFRINGEMENT?

Can an author infringe his own writings? By an odd coincidence, evangelist Billy Graham, author of some well-known books, was charged with that offense. Doubleday & Company, one of Graham's publishers, claimed that Graham's book "How to Be Born Again," published by Ward Books, Inc., contains several passages taken from Graham's "World Aflame," published by Doubleday.

Doubleday's legal counsel declared that even if the material in certain areas is not word for word, it is "thought for thought." A spokesman for Ward Books said, "Obviously there are only so many ways in which you can write or preach about the same beliefs you've held for so many years."

The Reverend Graham said he was surprised at the charge. Of course, he said, there are duplications — "my own preachings and quotations from the gospel." Besides, he added, "I own the copyrights in both books and I'll let the publishers work out a solution."

9

Copyright Registration

WORKS PROTECTED BY A UNITED STATES COPYRIGHT bear a formal notice consisting of three elements specified by the old as well as the new copyright act. The word "Copyright" is followed by the year of first publication and the name of the copyright owner, thus:

Copyright 1978 John Doe

The notice is placed on the title page of a book or on its reverse side. The symbol © in the copyright notice is recommended to authors who desire additional protection in countries which, like the United States, belong to the International Copyright Union. Such notices should read:

© 1978 John Doe

Phonorecords of sound recordings protected by United States copyrights also bear a three-element notice, consisting of the letter **P** in a circle, thus:

℗ 1978 John Doe

The omission of a formal copyright notice on copies or sound recordings does not invalidate the copyright in a work —

- **if the notice was omitted from a relatively-small number of copies or recordings distributed to the public**
- **if the copyright registration was made before publication of the work**
- **if the notice was omitted in violation of the copyright owner's written request**

If no name or date appear on copies or sound recordings distributed with the copyright owner's authority, the work is considered to have been published without a notice. Persons who innocently infringe the copyright because they were misled by the omission of a notice, may or may not be judged liable in an infringement suit.

The Copyright Act is adamant on a requirement that the owner of

COPYRIGHT EXAMINERS judge materials deposited by applicants for originality, eligibility and compliance with statutes. Left: Examiner reviews a microfilmed manuscript. Right: Music examiner listens to a sound recording.

INSIDE THE COPYRIGHT OFFICE

MILLIONS of indexed and bound copyright registrations are preserved in this reference library.

BOOK EXAMINER, left, inspects newly-published books on arrival. Applicants for registration are required to submit two copies of the "best edition." Operator of computer terminal, right, transmits data for the catalog of copyright entries.

PARTIAL VIEW of the extensive card file records section, one of the largest card file collections in the country.

any work published with a notice of copyright in the United States shall deposit within three months after the date of publication two complete copies of the best printed edition or two complete sound recordings of the best edition. Failure to comply may subject a copyright owner to a $250 fine for each work. Repeated refusals to meet the demand for copies may make the owner liable to an additional fine of $2500.

At any time during the existence of an unregistered copyright in a published or unpublished work, the owner may register his copyright claim by delivering to the Copyright Office two copies of the published work or one copy of an unpublished work, along with a completed Application for Registration of a Claim to Copyright and the appropriate fee. If the materials and documents deposited with the claim meet the statutory requirements, the Register of Copyrights will give the applicant a Certificate of Registration bearing an official seal.

The effective date of registration is the date on which a completed application, fee and copies or sound recordings are deposited in the Copyright Office. For the owner of a creative work, copyright protection constitutes a valuable precaution for security and peace of mind.

The vast number of privately-held unpublished works, formerly protected by State common laws, are now under Federal law, but their protection is limited to injunctions and the actual damage suffered. The owner of an unpublished work would receive full statutory rewards for infringements if, by registration, he makes a public record of his copyright.

In the case of a published work, no infringement action taken after the first publication of the work and before the effective date of its registration is eligible to receive awards, unless the registration was completed within three months after first publication of the work.

Service Fees Charged by the Copyright Office

For registering a copyright claim and the issuance of a Certificate of Registration $10.00

For registering a claim to renewal of a subsisting copyright still in its first term as of January 1, 1978 . . . . $ 6.00

For issuing a receipt for a deposit of copies or sound recordings . . . . $ 2.00

For recording the text of a transfer of copyright ownership or other document of six pages or less, covering just one title . $10.00

For making and reporting a search of Copyright Office records and for related services — each hour or fractional hour . $10.00

Fees for special services requiring a substantial amount of time and expense will be fixed by the Register of Copyrights.

10

Part Two
A NEW AGE FOR AUTHORS AND PUBLISHERS

Adjusting to the New Act

ALL ORIGINAL WORKS may receive Federal statutory copyright from the moment of their creation, without regard to when or whether they have ever been published. Creation (something the author does) supersedes publication (something the publisher or producer does) as the pivotal copyright act. The author is clearly identified in the statute as the first owner of copyright.

—Barbara Ringer
Register of Copyrights

AN EARLY ASSESSMENT OF THE NEW COPYRIGHT ACT leads to a belief that, on balance, it is a boon to authors, enhancing their juridical and professional status. It also opened a new chapter in the long struggle of authors to achieve equality with publishers in negotiating contracts.

Most important for every person embarking on a career of writing is the exclusive ownership of an original work for life plus 50 years, affording new and old authors added security and self-confidence. Next in importance is the copyright protection extended to works of authorship from their birth in a fixed form. Thus on January 1, 1978 uncounted millions of original unpublished manuscripts and other creative works acquired an unprecedented legal status. The author-owners of these works were free to claim Federal copyright registrations.

How many long-idle works will enter the marketplace remains to be seen. Whether they do or do not, their authors may find comfort and solace in the ownership of a useful but intangible asset — a copyright, the value of which often improves with age.

Next it is timely to consider how the new Act improves the status of authorship. It entitles authors to a virtually unrestricted lifelong deed to personal property even before its publication or distribution. This exclusive right or "monopoly" begins when an author's original creation crystallizes into a fixed form. Such legal support endows the owners with a posture of strength in negotiations with publishers and licensees, succinctly stated by Barbara Ringer, the Register of Copyrights:

"Certificates of copyright registration have been important to the bargaining position of authors of unpublished musical and dramatic works, even under the old Act; and the same may be true in the future with respect to authors of unpublished literary works."

In assessing their policies and goals under the new Act, publishers recognize the value and advantage to writers of copyright ownership before a manuscript is published. They see it as a challenge to their ingenuity and resourcefulness in surmounting a handicap and in negotiating profitable agreements.

Under the old Act, many authors were obliged to yield copyrights to publishers as a condition for getting their works into print. The power to print with copyright protection was the lever that moved mountains for publishers when *they* held the keys to copyrights.

By reversing almost two centuries of tradition, the new Act grants the author and creator an automatic copyright on completing an act of creation. Now authors approach editorial sanctums holding the keys to copyrights as well as the manuscripts. Even so, it is difficult to equate their respective roles since they deal in extremely variable commodities and resources.

The Challenge to Publishers

Many months before the new Act took effect, publishers were well-informed on its provisions. In seminars and conferences with legal advisers and lawmakers, they prepared themselves to deal with authors on the terms prescribed in Title 17, as amended.

Under the Act, the changes in publisher-author relations are significant. Before 1978, publishers asked for and usually received an exclusive license to publish and market an author's work for 28 years, that is, the first term of a copyright. However the single-term copyright for life plus 50 years may be more than many authors are willing to license. Both parties must agree on new time limits.

It appears that publishers will stiffen and amplify the language dealing with secondary and subsidiary rights which they are anxious to have. But under the new Act they must spell out their terms and conditions and bear in mind that an author's acceptance and his signature must be voluntary. Another change of attitude involves an author's unpublished manuscripts. The copyright of a handwritten or typewritten manuscript is equivalent to the Federal protection given to a printed work.

Some publishers may chafe under the provisions of Title 17 and seek to free themselves from its restraints by offering ready-made contracts to authors who may be willing to work as "employees for hire", that is, for wages or for lump-sum payments. It is doubtful whether established authors would accept such offers.

Publishers were ably represented by staff workers of the Association of American Publishers (AAP), participating in the legislative hearings and debates leading to the new Act. On some issues, such as non-compulsory licensing for non-commercial broadcasting and restraints on free photocopying, the AAP collaborated with the Authors League but on some other issues they held opposing views.

"Rampant Consumerism"

Thus the publishers were well-informed on the main problems and possible solutions but not completely satisfied with the results. A high AAP official characterized the new Act as ". . . . a negotiated cease-fire in a long twilight struggle between owners and users."

At the end, AAP leaders resolved to resist by all available means the "rampant consumerism" which demands free access to and the use of copyrighted works. As publishers, as well as copyright owners and licensees, they will seek legal remedies should their pleas to educators, librarians and others fail to curb the abuse of "free use" photocopying.

Under the new Act, AAP has inaugurated a system of clearances and permissions covering the use of non-dramatic literary works. With librarians and educators it has developed guidelines for photocopying that goes beyond "fair use". A Copyright Clearance Center with headquarters in New York City coordinates these activities.

The Technical, Scientific and Medical Division of AAP has presented to the National Commission on New Technological Uses of Copyrighted Works (CONTU) a technical photocopying proposal designed to meet the demands for copies of articles in scientific journals. The plan includes a coding system whereby users report their copying activities to a clearing house and payment center; the proceeds would be payable to copyright owners.

CONTU, a temporary agency attached to the Library of Congress, is involved in a deep study on the possible use of copyrighted works in computer systems capable of storing, retrieving and transferring information by various forms of machine reproduction. CONTU will expire after submitting its final report to Congress and the President.

FOR THE FIRST TIME IN AMERICAN LAW, the crucial facts surrounding the length of most copyrights will involve the identity and existence of the individual author rather than the activities of a publisher or producer in disseminating copies. The basic identification of copyright with the author rather than the publisher should in time affect the way people look at copyright law in general.

—Barbara Ringer
Register of Copyrights

11

Know Your Publisher

WHO IS YOUR PUBLISHER?

Knowing your publisher is not as easy as it appears to be or "used to be." In the halcyon days of independent publishing, hard-headed entrepreneurs like Messrs. Putnam, Liveright, Knopf, Appleton and Schuster made the bold decisions. Now decisions are often relayed to authors through layers and echelons of subordinates. The founders and builders of many publishing dynasties have passed to their reward, but their names emblazon a burgeoning book industry dominated by corporate empires.

Reminiscing on his career of half a century, during which he produced 52 books, author James T. Farrell mentioned the complications of being published. It was simplier when he started, he said. "A writer wrote and a publisher published. There were not as many agents and lawyers and discussions about paperback rights and film rights. A publisher wouldn't have thought of asking salesmen what the 'industry' reaction to a title would be. Even then, friendship between authors and publishers was uneasy at best. The artist and editor hear the sounds of distinctly different drums."

The New York Telephone Directory lists about 800 "book publishers", from guidebooks to encyclopedias, most of them relatively small. Others are scattered around the country. Many firms own "imprints", that is, books published under various house trademarks. Amidst a confusion of imprints, the conventional directories fail to reveal the massive consolidation movement spearheaded by industrial giants which, through mergers, takeovers and eliminations, have sharply reduced the number of viable and independent houses.

Leading corporations of the electronics industry have made a headlong plunge into the sea of publishing by courting and acquiring less affluent firms. Radio Corporation of America owns Random House, Alfred A. Knopf, Inc., Pantheon Books and Ballantine Books as well as the National Broadcasting Co.

On its part, the Columbia Broadcasting System controls two successful paperback firms, the Fawcett publishing interests and Popular Library. It also owns Holt, Rinehart & Winston and the Praeger Publishing Co. The CBS complex has expanded widely in Latin America and produces some 400 book titles annually.

International Telephone and Telegraph Co. owns the diversified G. K. Hall Publishing Co., the Bobbs-Merrill Co. and Who's Who.

Another publishing empire was carved out by Gulf + Western Industries which also owns Madison Square Garden and sugar plantations in the Dominican Republic. It took over the house of Simon & Schuster, Pocket Books, Inc. and a number of lesser publishing subsidiaries along with Paramount Pictures.

Music Corporation of America, parent of Universal Pictures, Inc., bought the publishing firms of G. P. Putnam Sons and Coward McCann and Geoghegan, accounting for several hundred book titles annually.

Appeal to the Government

Such developments, documented and amplified by long-range studies, prompted the Authors Guild and its Authors League affiliate to appeal to the Department of Justice and Federal Trade Commission to reverse an accelerating trend toward a concentration of power and the suppression of competition by conglomerate action.

In its brief entitled "The Continuing Trend of Power in the Book Publishing Industry", the Guild charged that a succession of more than 300 mergers, takeovers and eliminations in the past 20 years demonstrates that the "trend in the industry is to oligopoly." The appeal emphasized that the merger trend threatens competition in the indusry, restricts authors' bargaining power, income and publishing opportunities, endangers the public's access to a free marketplace of ideas and violates Section 7, the anti-merger clause, of the Clayton Act.

The surviving firms, it added, are seriously disadvantaged and ultimately may be forced to surrender to the conglomerates. Even now, a handful of conglomerates dominate and virtually control textbook and technical publishing. The statement urged Government authorities to order diverstitures and to prohibit further violations that endanger independently-owned publishing houses and undermine the livelihood of authors.

Conglomerate Alliances

Statistics make it clear that, directly or indirectly, the conglomerates dominate the hardbound and paperbound book industry, while the percentage of new books by independent publishers is steadily dwindling. With their power and wealth, the conglomerates woo the best-selling authors and mount national sales and promotional drives; without such means, the independents cannot compete.

Officers of the Guild pointed to the sinister effects of covert alliances and agreements between hardcover publishers, book clubs and paperback houses. Furthermore, they charged that trade publishers have compelled authors to surrender separate rights to license books to book clubs, paperback houses and others. Interlocking arrangements and discount practices within a financial complex shut out competition from independents. Most of the book clubs are owned, operated or managed by trade books publishers. Houses having the proper affiliations may dispose of large quantities of books through associated or integrated book clubs. Meanwhile the restrictions imposed on many cultural works deny the public's access to important books that are not "best-sellers."

The Conglomerate Way

"Obviously," the Guild's brief declared, "the publisher who controls paperback rights can license them to the house it has acquired (or to one owned by a common master) rather than to a competing publisher. The same threat exists when a trade publisher owns, is owned by or belongs to the owner of a book club, TV network or magazine."

The various collaborations and "tie-in" arrangements with publishing affiliates probably contravene the law. The control of an author's rights without his free consent violates the Copyright Act which, traditionally and currently, grants all original rights to the author.

The Guild's appeal won a response from Arizona Congressman Morris K. Udall, Wisconsin Congressman Robert W. Kastenmeier and 25 other members of the House who co-sponsored a Competition Review Act, covering industries suspected of hindering competition.

With corporate links and financial clout, the conglomerates have little competition but with each other. Eleven paperback houses control about 90 percent of the softbound book business.

Paperback revenues are steadily improving and in time they may surpass revenues from hardbound books. The prices paid for promising paperback titles have mounted accordingly. A publisher described the literary goldrush as "an all-or-nothing business." To stay in the race for bestsellers, a publisher can't afford to pay less than $100,000 per title.

The sharp bidding for paperback rights began in 1965 when Truman Capote's reportage of grim murder *In Cold Blood* was sold for $500,000. Seven years later, the reprint rights to Thomas A. Harris' *I'm Okay—You're Okay* were auctioned for a round million dollars. In 1973 *The Joy of Cooking* topped that when $1.5 million were paid for reprint rights. Recently Australian writer Colleen McCullough's novel *The Thorn Birds* fetched $1.9 million, leaving publishers and agents gasping, "What's next?"

Let it be known that some high bids for reprint rights are speculative and do not pay off. Also relatively few authors garner wealth by writing books. Six and seven-figure bids are neither indicative nor representative of authors' earnings. The odds still weigh heavily against

THE MASS MARKET for paperback books—an explosion in numbers.

serious middle authors with something important to say. For them, book publishers are often too busy to listen.

A leading publisher admitted that the trend is "to novels of what I would call commercial quality. We are gambling more on fewer titles." And an editor-in-chief acknowledged that conglomerate owners ". . . are interested only in the bottom line." (profit and loss).

A Reply from the Columbia Broadcasting System

A strong reaction to the charge that the big conglomerates are stifling competition and free enterprise came from John D. Backe, president of CBS, a major communications conglomerate.

Competition among the three television networks "has been a trial of fire for all of us," he said, ". . . and the result has been a bonanza for the viewers." He declared that the wave of mergers was a perfectly natural reaction to changing economic conditions. "Government intervention could very well be a foot in the door to Government intervention in the creative process itself. . . .

"I probably won't win over those who yell that the sky is falling every time some communications company merges with another. What so many media critics — both in and out of Government — really want is not diversity. What a lot of them want is to remove a thorn from their sides — a strong, independent and outspoken communications industry. They know that only big communications companies with extensive resources can properly report on, investigate and stand up to the powers of big business, big government and big labor," Backe said.

"The public's interest cannot be served if communications is relegated to a cottage-industry status in an age of industrial giants . . . the system we have built up over the years has done a better job for the population than any other yet devised. And until someone can show us something better, it deserves our full support."

Mr. Backe evidently sees a battle of the big conglomerates against the powers of big government, big business and big labor. Perhaps that explains why "cottage industries" like the Literary Guild, Book of the Month Club, Pocket Books, Inc., the Popular Library, Bantam Books, Simon & Schuster and G. P. Putnam Sons had to be taken over — to preserve their independence and diversity.

Apart from the takeovers of book publishers and book clubs, Congressman Udall has expressed concern over the elimination through mergers and takeovers of numerous family-owned dailies by introducing the Independent Local Newspaper Act, with endorsements from 34 other members of the House.

About 170 companies own 1050 (60 percent or almost two-thirds) of the 1700 dailies published in the United States, a situation with grave social and political implications. Udall does not consider all independent newspapers to be good nor all newspaper chains to be bad. But, he added, the trend toward bigness and absentee ownership signifies a real loss to society — the publisher with roots in the community. The family-owned newspaper is an "endangered species."

The devastating effect of estate taxes upon local newspaper owners is a major reason for selling out to the chains. Since their estates will not be able to pay estate taxes and maintain their newspaper properties as well, local owners make tax-free exchanges of their interest for the stock of newspaper chains and other properties.

If enacted, Udall's bill would provide tax relief for local newspaper owners by establishing an advance state tax payment trust, to be funded from corporate earnings; also he would defer estate tax payments for a reasonable period after the death of the owners.

IF ANY PERSON HAS A SOCIAL RESPONSIBILITY it is the publisher of books. For we face the loss of communications and an acute absence of ideas in almost every other medium, the principal culprit being concentration and lust for the dollar. Yours is a healthy industry . . . but earning reports are the siren song of concentration. An industry has the capability of monitoring its own trends and to warn against what may be attractive to the accountants, but may be bitter to society.

—Arizona Congressman Morris K. Udall
in an address before the
Association of American Publishers

12

Author-Publisher Contracts

FROM TIME TO TIME a publisher requests and receives an unrestricted publishing license and all subsidiary rights — the whole works. But experience teaches that when an author grants everything he usually receives less than a fair share of the rewards and profits.

In a standard book contract the author licenses a publisher to manufacture and market his work for a schedule of royalty payments prescribed in their agreement. Almost any original work has subsidiary rights which may be sold, leased, transferred or licensed, singly or collectively. If licensing agreements are concluded, the new Copyright Act makes it rather imperative for writers and publishers to record such agreements, both for published and unpublished works, since infringement suits must be supported by recorded instruments, giving *prima facie* evidence of the hard facts.

The "Tree of Rights"

Consider your original work as a tree whose trunk and branches are related but different. The "trunk" represents the primary license to a publisher to produce and market your work. The "branches" of this metaphorical tree represent secondary rights you may optionally license, either to your publisher, to other parties or reserve to yourself.

The grant of primary publication rights is a pure license which authorizes a publisher to manufacture and market the first and succeeding editions of a work. This license may be limited to a given term of years and prohibited from being assigned or transferred by the publisher without the author's written consent.

In granting a primary license, the author may add an authorization to negotiate the lease or sale of some or all secondary rights. Exercising his authority to sub-license, a publisher may, for example, sell translation rights in French, Spanish and German to firms in those respective countries. The author may specify time limits, say, from three to seven years, when rights that have not been sold may be recaptured by him.

In practice, while sub-licensing exclusive rights, the publisher, acting as the author's agent, is obliged to submit operational reports to the author (the principal) preferably on a quarterly basis but not less than semi-annually. His reports should identify sub-licensees and outline the terms of agreements. On request, a publisher should provide copies of individual sub-licenses to an author.

On-Time Payments to Authors

A publisher breaches a contract when he fails to remit an author's share of sub-licensing income on the dates agreed upon. Customarily publishers make reports and payments at six-month intervals, but some contracts call for payments within 30 days after the publisher receives any income from sub-licenses. Also some authors request direct payments from the sub-licensees themselves.

Publishers generally resist a writer's right to submit a contract proposal even as a basis for negotiation, saying, in effect, "We write the contracts because we pay out the money." Writing a book may consume years of an author's time, but unless it yields a profit, a writer's time and labor have no value to a publisher. Hence the weak bargaining position of new writers. Established authors wield the strongest clout to back up their contract demands.

A printed contract may look impressive but it is no more sacred than a handwritten or typewritten agreement. In whatever form, the contract is worthy of study and consideration since you may have to live with it for the rest of your days. Bear in mind that the text has been carefully contrived by a specialist who is dedicated to the publisher's profits, not to your profit or bid for fame. Naturally the publisher's interests receive preferential treatment in the contract.

Publishers observe that many authors and artists are motivated by lofty ideals; and they often lack business experience and are only vaguely familiar with calculating royalties, discounts and percentages. Publishers are prone to concede little in striking a bargain, while authors may yield to soft-spoken blandishments. If an author's eagerness to be published carries him away, a publisher may squeeze the juice out of his royalties and leave him with the residue.

Some authors prefer direct negotiations with publishers; others leave negotiations to lawyers and literary agents. No matter who participates, it is the author who must live with the contract; and his heirs may have to abide it too. The inference here is that authors are well-advised to be knowledgeable of the terms, obligations and *raison d'être* of an instrument so vital to their work and welfare. An author is entitled to know what he is getting in return for value given and should make his views known. Otherwise he may be obliged to accept terms and responsibilities which he cannot fulfill.

Most literary agents and copyright attorneys practice in metropolitan publishing centers, just a handful of cities across the country. Authors in small communities must rely on correspondence or the telephone.

All the more reason why persons engaged in creating original works should be versed in author-publishing contracts and vital provisions of the Copyright Act.

Contracts vary widely and each must be judged on its own merits. Bilateral agreements are supposed to reflect a meeting of the minds of the principals, arrived at through consultation and negotiation. The truth is that many contracts are concluded with an author's ready acceptance of the publisher's terms and little more than casual scrutiny and bargaining.

McGuffey's Big Mistake

Doubtless the celebrated author-educator William Holmes McGuffey (1800-1873) who compiled the six McGuffey's *Eclectic Readers,* prime learning tools for three generations of American children, was one of those trusting souls.

McGuffey's contract with his initial publisher, Truman and Smith of Cincinnati, allowed him a royalty of ten percent on each copy sold — that is, up to a maximum of $1000. Thereafter the copyright reverted to the publisher. Over the decades, McGuffey's readers chalked up sensational sales, totaling 122 million copies. The publisher had no cause to complain; but McGuffey, his family and friends, never forgot his big mistake.

A number of surveys and studies of author-publisher contracts have yielded data suggesting that many complaints about the unfairness of publishing contracts are justified. They help to explain why many creative writers receive deficient terms and inadequate earnings. A close look at their contracts reveals where some improvements can be made.

Some publishers evade the conventional contract wherein both parties contribute to an agreement. They simply send a letter to the author, saying, "This will confirm our agreement to publish a book written by you on the subject of ____________________ hereinafter known as the "work". Then the letter spells out terms and conditions allegedly agreed upon and concludes by saying, "If the foregoing correctly sets forth our agreement, please sign all copies of the agreement and retain one copy for yourself."

Unless an author had agreed in advance to the stated terms and precise language of that letter, he would be well-advised to consult a competent attorney and ascertain whether the letter offers a square deal or something else.

If the publisher's letter contains clauses or phraseology not previously discussed or agreed upon, it represents a denial of the author's right to participate in the formulation of terms and the choice of language in an agreement. Whether it is a personal letter or a formal printed contract, any publisher's offering should be considered as a proposal, subject to negotiation and revision.

Authors as "Employees for Hire"

Special clauses in the Copyright Act protect the authors of anonymous and pseudonymous works and "works made for hire". This last category refers to authors and other creators of original works who receive salaries, fees or other considerations for services rendered. Under the Act, all three categories may be protected by copyright for 100 years from the date of creation or 75 years from the date of publication, whichever is shorter.

Every person engaged in creative authorship should be aware of the legal committment and implication of the phrase "employee for hire" because it is a basic provision of the new Act as well as the old one. That simple phrase makes "authors" of non-writing publishers, promoters, agents, etc., and it may leave genuine authors virtually deprived and "holding the bag".

"Employee for hire" or "contractor for hire" and its twin phrase "works made for hire" should hoist red signals when they appear in an agreement. Although the Copyright Act declares that ". . . . the source of copyright ownership is the author of a work", it also upholds a legal principle that an author relinquishes his claim to the benefits and profits of a copyright if he works for a fee or salary or accepts commissions, assignments or orders to write a "work made for hire". In such cases, the employer is recognized as the legal "author" and copyright owner.

A firm may commission a writer to produce a book for a predetermined fee. The parties conclude a written agreement in which the writer is identified as an "employee for hire". Once the writer is paid for the completed assignment, he loses all proprietary rights and authorship because his employer is immediately eligible to register as the "author" and copyright owner.

The best-selling book *Elvis: What Happened?* was written by Steve Dunleavy, a salaried New York Post reporter, as an assignment from the Post's publisher. Allegedly Dunleavy taped 300 hours of interviews with three ex-bodyguards of the late rock artist Elvis Presley; they received $50,000 for the interviews. Dunleavy completed writing his manuscript just before Presley died and paperback book sales skyrocketed to an estimated five million copies with a retail price tag of $1.95 each. Publisher Rupert Murdock of the Post and Ballantine Books, Inc. reaped princely profits. So far as known, writer Dunleavy received just his wages.

Another example of an "employee for hire" who made millions for his employer and considerably less for himself concerns author-professor Eric Segal. In 1969 Paramount Pictures paid Segal $50,000 for the motion picture script of *Love Story* and it became one of the ten best box-office hits of all time. Learning from that experience, Segal sold his script for *Oliver's Story,* a sequel to *Love Story,* for $1,500,000.

Any author signing an agreement in which he is identified as an "employee" or "contractor for hire" can forget all claims to profits from his work except the consideration agreed upon in a written instrument. Bear in mind that the Copyright Act defines a work made for hire as one "prepared by an employee within the scope of his or her employment." It may also be a work or service performed by anyone hired especially for a given task. A self-employed artist or a free lance writer identified as "an "employee for hire" in a signed agreement lose copyright protection because an employer's proprietary rights supersede the rights of "employees for hire."

To prevent fraud or deception, the Act provides a safety valve: In applying for copyright registration, the claimant (an employer in this case) must state that he is seeking to protect a "work made for hire". If the claimant is not the original author, he must state how he obtained ownership of the work.

A Variation of the "Employee" Theme

Some book reprint houses have been known to originate ideas for books, pre-sell them to film companies and then provide monetary advances to selected authors who undertake the writing. In such situations, the author must make sure he is not sacrificing the title to his copyright or to his book's primary and secondary rights.

Four Relevant Dates

From an author's view, four working dates are relevant to a publishing agreement:

- **The date of contract signing, signifying that the parties have reached a mutually-satisfactory agreement**
- **The date when the author's completed manuscript is due for delivery. The contract may say ". . . . on receipt of a manuscript acceptable to the publisher"**
- **A 30 to 60-day interim, after which the "acceptability" clause in the contract would be void**
- **The publication date of the first trade edition — less than one year after the contract signing**

A monetary advance on the book may be payable in a lump sum to the author on the signing date, or in installments payable up to the date of publication.

A publisher may want to bind an author to a completed manuscript delivery date, but himself decline to fix a publication date. Both dates may have 30 to 60-day grace periods to cover delays beyond control of the parties.

In these days of mergers and reorganizations, editorial directors frequently change. What is "acceptable" to one may be anathema to his successor.

A cash advance to the author on signing an agreement may symbolize "acceptance" of his manuscript and forestall later demands for extensive revisions. However, if an author makes revisions that are still "unacceptable", he is in a precarious position. Publishers have also been known to lose faith in a book's sales potential after signing an agreement. Unless such contingencies are resolved, an author may decide to keep the cash advance as a "kill" fee and seek another publisher.

In effect, the advance paid by a publisher is considered a non-refundable option price paid for an exclusive right to publish the author's work. The only valid reason for refunding an advance would be the author's failure to deliver a complete manuscript on the contract date.

Copyright Infringements

Most contracts establish procedures for preventing infringements. The copyright may belong to the author of a work but its defense is the publisher's primary responsibility since he holds an exclusive license which is jeopardized in case an infringement is not enjoined. However, rewards or damages arising out of a negotiated settlement or litigation should be shared with the author.

Under the new Act, unpublished works are also protected by copyrights, but their defense is the responsibility of the owners.

AUTHOR, BEWARE OF ——

PUBLISHERS who refuse to negotiate terms.

PUBLISHERS who refuse to write into a contract a fixed date for publishing your work.

CONTRACTS which refer to you as an "employee for hire," or "contractor for hire" or similar appelations, that is, if you are NOT an employee, contractor, agent or on a paid assignment.

CONTRACTS which omit the specific title of your work or at least a "working title" subject to later negotiation and mutual agreement.

CONTRACTS which assume a legal title to or control of any exclusive right to your work without your written consent or without stipulation of royalties or other compensation. Such rights belong to the author and should be negotiated separately from royalties for book sales through retail channels.

CONTRACTS which provide a negligible amount as a cash advance and sub-standard royalty schedules — unless, for good reason, they are negotiated to your satisfaction.

CONTRACTS which omit fixed dates for paying royalties and the author's share of income from all licenses and sub-licenses. Such payments, accompanied by factual reports, should be made at least semiannually.

"UNILATERAL AGREEMENTS" wherein an author is asked to affix his signature to a letter dictated by a publisher or his representative. Insist on a two-party (bilateral) contract wherein your name and identity and the publisher's name and identity are clearly established as parties to the contract.

CONTRACTS which fail to specify where and when the first English language edition of your work will be manufactured and sold.

CONTRACTS which deny the author's exclusive authority to assign, license or terminate his secondary rights after a term of years. Neither should contracts abrogate the author's right to negotiate exclusive licenses on his own behalf.

A PUBLISHER who files a claim for copyright registration of your work without your written authorization.

The Indemnity Clause

The author's indemnity clause is the most serious and sensitive committment he makes in a publishing contract. For here he agrees to pay damages to a plaintiff if a court rules against the author and publisher. However, unless a contract stipulates it, a publisher may not withhold an author's royalties as payment for damages decreed by a court.

Understandably, the insurance companies that insure publishers decline to insure authors. On sensitive and borderline passages in a manuscript, it is helpful to seek guidance and counsel from an expert in libel law.

It is proper to safeguard a publisher against any claim brought against him by reason of libelous or unlawful matter in an author's work. The author customarily guarantees that he is the sole writer and proprietor of the work and owns all the rights licensed to the publisher; and that to be best of his knowledge his work does not infringe or violate any right of any person. The author's liability should be limited to damages actually paid by the publisher in a suit against the publisher, after appeals are exhausted.

The Bankruptcy Clause

Usually omitted in a contract, an author should request the inclusion of a clause saying, in effect, that if the publisher is adjudicated a bankrupt or makes an assignment for the benefit of creditors or liquidates the publishing business, his agreement with the author shall terminate and all rights thereto shall automatically revert to the author.

Assignments, Takeovers and Mergers

Since change is a durable feature of human affairs, publishing houses, even as authors and artists, must anticipate the day when they may wish to sell, assign or bequeath rights, properties and holdings to others.

Any such assignment and transfer privilege authorized for a publisher and denied to the author should alert the author to an injustice. To prevent what may amount to virtual expropriation or to being "sold down the river", the author should request rights and privileges identical to those which the publisher takes for himself. To equate benefits and responsibilities, both parties should have equal rights to assign or transfer, either freely or by mutual consent.

Restoring a Book Out-of-Print

Among authors there is a preference for a six to nine-month grace period for reprinting a book after it goes out of print. Some authors request contract clauses which provide for a cancellation of non-licensed rights six or nine months after a book goes out of print, if the publisher has failed to restore it.

The Ethic of Simultaneous Submissions

In years gone by, publishers frowned on writers who practiced simultaneous submission, that is, sending manuscripts simultaneously to more than one publisher. This was necessary because many publishers "sat" on submitted manuscripts for months at a time. But now that publishers conduct manuscript auctions to which they invite six or more competitive bidders, the ethic of multiple submissions needs no further justification.

The Free Copy Clause

In a customary gesture among publishers, an author receives "gratis" ten copies of his published work. Thereafter he may purchase copies at the usual 40 percent discount from the catalog list price that publishers give to dealers.

Authors' Alteration Clause

Alterations to printers' proofs in excess of ten percent of the cost of composition are chargeable to authors. The hourly rate charge for metropolitan printers is at an all-time high.

Concluding the Author-Publisher Agreement

Many contracts close with a statement that the text constitutes the entire understanding between the parties and may not be modified or amended except by a written and signed agreement by both parties.

13

Rights and Royalties

NEVER UNDERESTIMATE THE VALUE OF SECONDARY RIGHTS to an original work. The new Act places major emphasis on an author's ownership and control of these rights as well as of primary rights.

Accordingly, publishers have adapted their operations and plans to a requirement for seeking an author's consent before carrying out certain exploitation programs and activities. "The Act," says Copyright Register Barbara Ringer, "has scrapped some bureaucratic thinking and shifted its philosophical base, ultimately providing support for further reforms."

Publishers are well aware that an author's exclusive right to secondary rights takes precedence over all other claims. Any assignment or transfer of a right must be spelled out over an author's signature. Likewise, a publisher may not sell rights to another publisher or file a claim to copyright registration without an author's written consent.

As authors familiarize themselves with the copyright provisions, they may feel inclined to participate actively in assigning and licensing rights because any transfer or lease carried out under pressure on the author will not be honored. An author is free to make independent decisions regarding the disposition of his bundle of rights and determine to what extent it is prudent to assign licenses to given firms and individuals.

Merchandising Secondary Rights

The management and merchandising of secondary rights has become a complex business, giving rise to entrepreneurs with expertise in various fields, especially in negotiating licenses for paperback books and performance rights — stage, TV, radio and motion pictures. In view of this specialization and of the opportunities at stake, established authors are licensing secondary rights to firms and individuals with professional skills and qualifications.

Whereas trade book publishers were often given the complete bundle of secondary rights, the present trend is to yield them the rights which most closely supplement their main activity, namely, producing and marketing printed works. In keeping with this trend, publishers are likely to receive exclusive licenses for paperback, book club, foreign and translation rights; also digests and first and second serial rights.

Royalties — The Author's Share of Profits

For an author, the royalty schedules for secondary rights lie at the heart of a publishing contract and bring forth the fruit of his labor.

If you conceive and produce a fixed original work independently, you are entitled to a fair share of the earnings. Your fair share is "royalty." In days of yore "royalty" was the perquisite of kings, the royal percentage taken on coins minted or precious metals mined. Authors, however, earn royalties by their originality and creativity. In plain prose, Noah Webster tells us that, "Royalty is a share of the profits received by the owner for permitting another to use his property." Specifically, he adds, ". . . . it is compensation paid to the owner of a copyright for the use of it or the right to act under it." Webster's definition sheds light on what a modern author is — the originator and proprietor of a copyrightable work.

Royalties on Book Sales

Based on publishers' retail catalog prices, the standard royalties now prevailing on hardcover trade books are:

10 percent on the first 5000 copies
12½ percent on the next 5000 copies
15 percent on all additional copies

Best-selling authors of hardcover trade books frequently receive royalties of 15 percent on copies sold at retail; lesser-known authors and artists may receive as little as five percent. On sales to big-quantity discount book merchandisers, the reduced profit margins on wholesale prices and royalties are generally authorized by contract clauses.

Surveys by the Authors Guild of America shows that:

- **About 14 percent of hardcover trade book contracts provide a straight 15 percent royalty on retail sales**
- **More than 90 percent of such contracts provide fixed royalties based on retail list prices**
- **These surveys also reveal that 2.3 percent of contracts call for royalties based on "wholesale" prices, i.e., the publishers' net receipts**

The Guild's surveys have focused on hardcover trade books. With the more specialized academic, textbook and scholarly books, a larger proportion of authors receive royalties calculated on a publisher's net receipts.

Various contracts specify a fixed royalty on each book sold, graduating upward with increased sales. In such cases, the author's earnings may drop far below standard royalty levels. Unless extenuating circumstances dictate an acceptance, it is advisable to stand firm by your request for the standard scale. Some publishers may offer sub-standard royalties to test an author's will and resistance, but may raise their minimum substantially if an author negotiates earnestly.

Bargain and negotiate for the best terms, and unless driven by necessity, an author should settle for nothing less than standard royalties. A retreat threatens the income and livelihood of your fellow authors.

Marketing Paperback Rights

Most trade books offer possibilities for licensing secondary rights and among the most important are paperback editions. The mass market for paperbound books has mushroomed, netting substantial profits for the leading houses, most of which are well-integrated into the big conglomerates.

Until the conglomerates absorbed the major paperback firms, the bidding for best-selling books and manuscripts by big-name writers was spirited and competitive. The conglomerates are likely to eliminate much of the high bidding by cornering the best-sellers owned by the conglomerates themselves or by affiliated enterprises. The smaller and independent paperback houses lack the means to enter high bids. However, some sensational or newsworthy books may still fetch six-figure bids.

Authors generally license paperback rights to their publishers or agents and may fix termination dates for such authorizations, in accordance with a trend to grant all rights for a given term of years, after which they revert to the owners.

The winning bid prices paid for paperback rights have stirred wide interest. Auction bids for single books have passed the million-dollar mark, proof of their profitability to publishers and to a few authors.

Some paperback houses reverse the usual publishing sequence by contracting for books ahead of hardcover publishers, then selling hardcover rights for a commission and paying the author a standard paperback royalty of six to eight percent on sales up to 150,000 copies.

A hardcover publisher usually receives 10 to 15 percent commission for auctioning off paperback rights. But for a conventional sale of rights by a publisher, the author may receive 50 percent of the proceeds on the first 10,000 copies and progressively more on subsequent sales.

First and Second Serial Rights

Established authors with press experience and contacts may prefer to retain first serial rights, which refer to installments or chapters published in newspapers or magazines prior to a book's publication date. If a publisher or author's agent negotiates the sale of first serial rights, they would be entitled to a ten percent commission. The same payment would apply to the sale of second serial rights, sold after a book's publication date. A three-year license term is considered adequate for selling second serial rights.

Book Club Rights

Book clubs, of which there are more than 100 in the United States, long provided a steady income and competitive market for outstanding literary works; but all that has changed now that conglomerates have taken over the major book clubs. Doubtless they will favor the books in which they own both primary and secondary rights.

Ordinarily publishers handle an author's book club rights on a 50-50 split of the proceeds. On bulk sales to book clubs, the author's royalties are only a fraction of his earnings from retail sales. The 50-50 split arrangement actually accounts to less, since the publisher may siphon off his expenses and overhead costs.

Performance Rights — Stage, TV, Radio and Motion Pictures

Performance rights are usually considered alien to a publisher's expertise and hence established authors prefer to parcel these out to agents with business connections in the ramified entertainment field. Authors who enjoy such connections reserve performance rights to themselves and retain all the income. Regardless of who an author may license to sell performance rights, authors customarily receive 90 percent of the proceeds, with the balance going to the firm or agent who negotiates the sale.

A classic example of a writer receiving a comparative pittance for valuable performance rights concerns Margaret Mitchell, author of *Gone With the Wind.* The motion picture rights to that work were sold to David Selznick for $50,000. Through the year 1975, the film grossed some $120 million — of which the author received an estimated net of $24,000 during her lifetime.

After her death at age 49 in an auto accident, the book's first term of copyright expired and, by law, her executors obtained the exclusive right to renew her copyright. Hence Metro Goldwyn Mayer, the distributor firm, had to apply to the executors for a renewal of the license. They obtained it but this time the royalty fee reflected the true value of the property. Had Margaret Mitchell lived, she would have received no more than $24,000 for the motion picture rights.

The Mitchell case and others similar to it explain why knowledgeable authors reserve motion picture and other performance rights to themselves. And for good reason, they are averse to a 50-50 split of the proceeds from performance rights. Of course, few books or plays can match the enormous popularity of *Gone With the Wind* but it behooves authors to anticipate at least a modicum of success for their work.

Foreign and Translation Rights

These related rights concern the distribution and sale of English language books in various areas overseas and foreign language versions in countries where translations are required for the predominant population. Many American authors have won loyal followings in foreign lands.

Although some publishers receive a 50-50 split of the income from foreign sales, established authors receive up to 75 percent of the net proceeds. Some American publishers are represented by foreign agents who may also demand a commission. To avoid double commissions and expense deductions, authors should opt for 75 percent of the gross proceeds from foreign sub-licenses. The author's grant of a foreign license should be revocable after a reasonable term of years.

Miscellaneous Rights

Rights concerned with comic books, film strips and other uses involved with graphics and reading matter are generally licensed to publishers; more specialized licenses are granted to firms and individuals with expertise in various forms of mass merchandising.

Remember the "Net"

Those little but ominous words "net" and "net proceeds" mean that a publisher plans to deduct his expenses, losses and overhead from your royalties on book sales and secondary rights, charging the author for his cost of doing business.

OBITUARY RECORDS IN THE COPYRIGHT OFFICE

THERE IS NO LONGER A FIXED DATE for the expiration of a copyright; it depends on an owner's life-span plus 50 years. For this reason the Register of Copyrights maintains obituary records on a current basis.

About 75 years after the first date of publication of a work, any person who receives from the Copyright Office a certified report that the records disclose nothing to indicate that the author of the work is living, or died less than 50 years before, "is entitled to rely upon a presumption" that the author has been dead for at least 50 years. Reliance in good faith upon this presumption shall be a complete defense to any action for infringement.

APPENDIX

Official Copyright Records

At periodic intervals the Copyright Office compiles and publishes catalogs and indices of all copyright registrations. It also maintains records of deposits and recordations. Such records are open to public inspection, subject to fees for copies thereof and for the services of employees engaged in searches.

Copyright deposits are maintained as long as possible but, under appropriate safeguards, they may be disposed of when the responsible officials decide it is necessary to do so.

The National Television and Radio Archives

In addition to its vast deposits of copyrighted literary, pictorial and musical works, the Library of Congress has established the National Television and Radio Archives to preserve the nation's television and radio heritage.

The Archives will seek to acquire "fixations" of TV and radio programs which have present or potential public, cultural or historical significance. Many such recorded programs have been deposited in the Library in connection with copyright registrations. Other programs will be acquired through trading or purchase. Also, under an amendment to the Copyright Act, the Library is authorized to tape programs off the air and may "demand" of broadcasters a copy or phonorecord of a particular program. Broadcasters have the option of meeting a "demand" by gift, by loan for reproduction or by sale at cost.

Termination of the "Manufacturing Clause"

The so-called "manufacturing clause", added to the copyright law in 1891, required English language books or periodicals to be manufactured in the United States in order to receive full copyright protection.

The new Act liberalized this provision after Congressional committees concluded it had outlived its usefulness. Accordingly until July 1, 1982, when the "manufacturing clause" will be nullified, the Act permits the importation of 2000 copies manufactured in all countries; however, this restriction does not apply to Canada or to works by Americans living abroad for more than one year.

Reproductions for the Blind and Handicapped

Under the new Act, the Copyright Office has established forms and procedures whereby copyright owners may voluntarily grant, without receiving payments or fees, a license to the Library of Congress, permitting certain broadcasts and the reproduction and distribution of copies in Braille and phonorecords for the sole use of the blind and physically handicapped persons.

Protection of Foreign Authors

Unpublished original works by foreign authors may be registered in the Copyright Office and protected under United States law, irrespective of the nationality or residence of the copyright owners.

However a United States copyright does not cover a published work unless one or more of the authors is an American national or a resident of the United States; or is a resident national of a country that is party to a copyright treaty to which the United States is also a signatory; or is a stateless person residing in any part of the globe.

A clause in the new Act prevents foreign governments from expropriating the United States copyrights of their respective nationals.

International Copyright Protection

The rapid increase in literary and artistic production, coupled with swift communications and a freer exchange of ideas has created new overseas markets for original works of authorship.

Many countries have concluded reciprocal agreements with the United States through the Universal Copyright Convention, the Pan American Copyright Convention and the Convention for the Protection of Producers of Phonograms. Additionally the United States maintains bilateral copyright relations with various countries, by virtue of treaties or proclamations.

The countries currently maintaining copyright relations with the United States are:

Algeria
Andorra
Argentina
Australia
The Bahamas
Bangladesh
Belgium
Bolivia
Brazil
Bulgaria
Cambodia
Cameroon
Canada
Chile
China
Colombia
Costa Rica
Cuba
Czechoslovakia
Denmark
Dominican Republic
Ecuador
El Salvador
Fiji
Finland
France
Germany
Ghana
Greece
Guatemala
Haiti
Honduras
Hungary
Iceland
India
Ireland
Israel
Italy
Japan
Kenya
Laos
Lebanon
Liberia
Liechtenstein
Luxembourg
Malawi
Malta
Mauritius
Mexico
Monaco
Morocco
Netherlands
New Zealand
Nicaragua
Nigeria
Norway
Pakistan
Panama
Paraguay
Peru
Philippines
Poland
Portugal
Romania
Senegal
South Africa
Soviet Union
Spain
Sweden
Switzerland
Tunisia
United Kingdom
Uruguay
Vatican City
Yugoslavia
Zambia

CREDITS

FRONT COVER ART by John R. Pack. Sketches on pp. 6, 7 and 8 by the author after Mountford, Moorhouse, Kuhn and Texaco Magazine. Maya glyphs, p. 9, from the Smithsonian Bureau of Ethnology; "Kipu" drawing from the author's collection. Gutenberg illustrations on pp. 11, 12, 13 from the Smithsonian's Graphic Arts Division and Library of Congress. Portrait of Queen Anne, p. 15, from William and Mary College. Title page of *The Whole Booke of Psalmes,* p. 17, from Library of Congress.

Drawing on p. 18 from John Clyde Oswald. Webster's Blue-Back Speller and portrait by Edwin B. Child, p. 19, are from G. & C. Merriam Co., Inc. The other Webster portrait is from Emily Ford's biography. *The Philadelphia Spelling Book,* p. 21, from Library of Congress.

Sculpture, on p. 24, from the New York World's Fair of 1939. Robida drawings, pp. 25, 26, 27, are from the author's collection. Photos of Morse, Berliner and Marconi, pp. 28 and 29, are from Library of Congress; Thomas Edison from General Electric Co. Photos on pp. 31 and 32 from American Telephone and Telegraph Co.

Portrait of Ben Franklin, p. 41, from James Parton's biography. Manual alphabet and finger talking, p. 42, from National Association of the Deaf and Gallaudet College. Illustrations on p. 44 from IBM. Photo of command post, p. 45, from RCA. Photos on p. 48 from Communications Satellite Corporation; on p. 49 from Dow, Jones & Co. Inc.

Photos of Leonard Bernstein and George Balanchine, pp. 51 and 53, from Richard Braaten; Artur Rubinstein, p. 52, from Sol Hurok, Inc. Drawing on p. 63 from Library of Congress. Photo of Arena Stage, p. 74, by Joe Mann. Charts on pp. 10 and 42, drawings of the Authors' Tree of Rights and the Copyright Comet and photos on pp. 36, 43, 46, 55, 56, 57, 58, 60, 62, 72, 73. 78, 79, and 87 are by the author. The "Cyclops" Space Telescope on the Back Cover is from Lockheed Aircraft Corporation.

AUTHOR OF THE TEN COMMANDMENTS